D1094160

BONNER & PARTNERS

WHEN THE ATMs GO DARK

How to Survive the End of America's 30 Year Credit Boom

About Bonner & Partners

Over time, the patterns of history tend to repeat themselves. Our goal is to put our subscribers on the right side of history, even if it should take years before it becomes obvious.

— Bill Bonner

Bonner & Partners is a financial publishing group based in Delray Beach, Florida. It was founded by Bill Bonner and his son Will in 2009 as the culmination of Bill's nearly four decades in the financial research business.

Bill founded the worldwide research network The Agora in 1979. Analysts at the group, including Bill himself, have exposed and predicted some of the world's biggest shifts since that time, starting with the fall of the Soviet Union back in the late '80s, and recently the election of President Trump.

Bonner & Partners focuses on noticing what the mainstream media ignores. Its everyday mission is to help you look behind the curtain of Wall Street and Big Government and prepare you for big changes before they happen.

Since its founding, Bonner & Partners has recruited a group of all-star analysts, including a former corporate banker who outperformed Warren Buffett and Carl Icahn over a 10-year period, as well as a former tech CEO turned active angel investor. They serve 115,838 readers, including 97,563 paying private subscribers.

Contents

Foreword 9

Part 1 – In the Ruins of America

Chapter 1: Dispatch from an Isolated Mountain Ranch 21

Chapter 2: Dead Flamingos 25

Chapter 3: Other People's Money 33

Chapter 4: What We Paid For 37

Chapter 5: Ruins 41

Chapter 6: A Nation of "Stable-Fed" Animals 45

Chapter 7: Cutting in Line 47

Part 2 – The Great Lie

Chapter 8: Something Went Wrong on the Way to the Future 55

Chapter 9: In the Beginning 59

Chapter 10: A New Money in America 61

Chapter 11: What Went Wrong at the Turn of the Century 65

Chapter 12: The Great Lie 69

Part 3 – The Great American Credit Collapse

Chapter 13: Cash Will Disappear......................................75

Chapter 14: When the Money Goes Bad 83

Chapter 15: The Road We're Following............................91

Chapter 16: Why Are We In This Mess?...........................99

Chapter 17: Deflation Works!...105

Chapter 18: Don't Expect the Fed to Sit Tight...............113

Part 4 – On Surviving (and Prospering) in the Age of Dying Credit

Chapter 19: Crisis Money Guide 119

Chapter 20: Cash Alternative: Gold Jewelry 123

Chapter 21: How to Own Gold 127

Chapter 22: Alternative Mediums of Exchange..............131

Chapter 23: Financial Secrets of the Resistance............145

Chapter 24: Keeping Your Money
from the Government (Legally) 149

Chapter 25: Your Secret, Legal, and Safe Overseas
Wealth Store (and How It Can Also Make You Rich) 155

Chapter 26: How a Gold Bug Almost Learned to
Love Cryptocurrencies… And Why Bitcoin Is Important Now 161

Chapter 27: Should I Be Investing? 183

Chapter 28: Living Overseas 193

Part 5 – Endgame

Chapter 29: The Final Act.. 215

Chapter 30: How to Keep Up with the
Latest in Bill's Investigation.. 219

Foreword

It's 5:37 p.m....

There's a cold sweat on the back of your neck...

You're standing at a payment terminal in a crowded grocery store...

A few yards away, the cashier's drumming her long red nails on the counter, next to your groceries. There's a long line of people waiting to pay.

You turn back to the payment terminal and swipe your card for the third time... Nothing happens...

Behind you, someone in the line lets out an exasperated sigh... you apologize to the cashier...

Annoyed, you head back to your car, where you fish out your cell phone and give the bank a call.

It takes three tries till a woman's voice finally answers...

But it's just a pre-recorded message... so garbled that you can't make out a word.

You hang up and start your engine....

On the way home, you stop off at the gas station...

The attendant comes out as usual, but before you can speak, he asks a strange question:

"You buying or selling?"

Confused, you tell him you just want to fill 'er up, but when you try to give him your credit card, he suddenly backs away...

"Sorry, we're closed, man... Sorry."

You sit there for a moment, wondering whether you should argue with the guy... Finally, you just head home.

You tell your wife what happened... Definitely strange... but she figures it's probably just a computer problem at the bank... They'll have it sorted out by morning...

You agree, but as you fall asleep later that night, you're not so sure...

Suddenly it's 4 a.m.... and there's a cold fear deep in the pit of your stomach...

Something doesn't feel right... If it's just a computer problem... The bank would have called you... But instead there was that strange message...

And what about that gas station attendant...?

First thing next morning, you take a trip to the bank... It doesn't look open.

A piece of paper taped to one of the doors tells you that it has been temporarily closed. No explanation... just a phone number to call and what looks like a government logo... but not one you recognize.

You give the number a shot... it's that garbled message again... You hang up.

Around the side of the building, there are a couple of dented ATMs with broken screens.

As you head back to your car, you notice a man kneeling down by a pickup truck parked nearby... He's got a hose running from the truck's gas tank into a jerry can.

Suddenly he looks up and catches you staring at him... The look in his eyes tells you not to linger... He watches as you get in your car and drive off.

Everything's closed... It's that same piece of paper everywhere... and the same dark screens on every ATM.

You start running into other people... trying to deposit social security checks... or take out cash... or find out why their cards suddenly aren't working.

This is not just a problem with your bank... Your whole town is essentially shut down...

By the time you call off the search and head home, Main Street is jammed with traffic. You take an alternate road... it leads you past the gas station from yesterday...

It's closed now... with a big chain across the entrance...

Inside, you see a pickup truck next to one of the pumps... Four men are standing around it... One of them is holding a crowbar...

Your wife's relieved as you walk through the door. Apparently people have been coming by all day... asking if she's got any cash... trying to sell her things...

And they're not people from the neighborhood, either.

You turn on the TV... but all you see are the same images of closed banks... smashed store windows... and talk of some kind of "crisis"... No one really knows what's happening...

And then your screen goes blue. Text at the center reads: "Service Interrupted: Please Update Payment Info."

You shut off the TV and go look out the window...

Your wife wonders aloud whether you should invite the neighbors over... You agree... This is looking like a time to stick together...

The sun is starting to set. The dark outline of a helicopter skims along the horizon...

You can't deny it anymore... This is it... The beginning of something you've expected for a long time now...

Except that you never really knew when... or what form it would take...

And maybe you even gradually stopped believing it would come at all...

Except now, it's here...

And as you stare into the coming night, you wonder how long the food in the pantry will last... and what you might have to do if this situation doesn't get resolved quickly...

***

What you are about to read is not about the end of the world.

It is not a prepper manual.

This is a book about a great myth... a great lie... and a decades-long experiment in the manipulation and perversion of American money, American minds, and American life.

Let's start with what we know for certain...

We know that, for the past 40-odd years, I have spent my career watching the greatest increase in debt in the history of the world. In 5,000 years of economic history, what is being attempted here in America is truly without equal.

We know the origins of our present situation. It began with an experiment kicked off decades ago, when I was a young man. We can trace all the strange ways in which this experiment dripped deeply into our society, warping our sense of who we are and what we are owed.

We also know that there seem to be patterns throughout history. These patterns, like fundamental laws of nature, may only be ignored at your peril. For our purposes, there are two patterns worth knowing.

The first is what we call "reversion to the mean," or "R2tM" for short.

As economists describe it, reversion to the mean is merely a recognition of the tendency for things to stay in a range that we recognize as "normal."

Trees do not grow 1,000 feet high. People don't run 100 mph. You don't get something for nothing.

Normal exists because things tend to follow certain familiar patterns, shapes, and routines.

When people go out in the morning, they know, generally, whether to wear a winter coat or a pair of shorts. The temperature is not 100 degrees one day and zero the next.

Occasionally, of course, odd things happen. And sometimes, things change in a fundamental way. But, usually, when people say "this time is different"... it's time to bet on normal.

This phenomenon – reversion to the mean – has been thoroughly tested and studied in the investment world. It seems to apply to just about everything – stocks, bonds, strategies, markets, sectors... you name it.

It also applies to nations.

Around 500 B.C., Rome was a riverside town of little significance with sheep grazing on its hills. Then the Romans conquered the known world, invented the toilet, and built the finest city ever seen.

By A.D. 500, Rome had returned to being a riverside town of little significance, with sheep grazing among the toppled columns.

We could go on, but the Book of Genesis (3:19) put it best when it said, "for dust thou art, and unto dust shalt thou return."

Put simply: What goes up will most assuredly come down.

The second fundamental law is called *hormesis*. I wrote a book about this phenomenon not long ago called *Hormegeddon*. For our purposes now, we can summarize this rule quickly as follows: Too much of a good thing leads to disaster.

All this is to say that if you look closely enough, as I have been doing for about 40 years now, history provides certain fundamental rules, as tried and true as the law of gravity. As we go forward, let's remember those two:

1. R2tM: When things get "out of whack," the best bet is that they will get back into whack soon.

2. *Hormesis*: One drink may be good for you; three or more will probably do more harm than good.

Such are the facts. They constitute what we know for certain.

Our purpose here is not to scare or sensationalize. No, we aren't going to tell you to sell all your stocks, or move to a bunker.

If we seem alarmist, it is only because the subject matter itself is alarming.

Our hope in putting together this book is to open your eyes to the grave danger looming over every single American's head... how it came to be and who created it... and the various ways you might survive its logical conclusion...

After that, you'll have to make choices that make sense for you.

I can only urge you to not act rashly, but to practice care and always remember to hedge your bets...

Make no mistake: It does not matter how smart or well informed you are; no one knows exactly how the future will unfold.

Who will stumble first: our credit card networks, D.C., Wall Street, or the suckers who took out auto loans to buy electric cars?

Some pundits (and a good many investment analysts!) like to say they know precisely when and how it all begins. Maybe one of them will get it right. But we have no way of knowing in advance which of them it will be... and neither do they.

Here we make a brief digression to talk business. It often happens that some would-be critic, eager to prove that he's no dupe, asks us the following three "gotcha" questions:

First, if you're so smart, how come you're not rich?

Well, actually we are "rich" by most standards. Not filthy rich... not billionaires. But we are quite comfortable.

Second, if you really could predict the financial future, why bother to tell me about it?

Well, for starters, we don't claim to predict the future. We are not running a psychic hotline. We just lay out what we see happening. As you will see, it is scary enough to cause alarm. And it should cause you to take some basic precautions, which I'll explain.

But don't get me wrong: I'm not Mother Teresa. This is no charity... and I'm not doing this for the "good of the world." This is how we earn our living: by studying the trends and events that the "mainstream" would rather ignore. Sometimes we're right. Sometimes we're wrong. But since your retirement, your wealth...

maybe even your safety... is at stake, it's worth taking a few minutes to pay attention.

If you think we're right about this, we hope you'll continue doing business with us for decades to come. It's that simple. No hidden agenda. Either you think it is worth the money or you don't. You decide.

> Third, you say the sky is falling, but other analysts in your group say this is a great time to invest.

Let me clarify. Nowhere in this book will you read that the sky is falling. Our premise is simply that economic trends and events have a real-world impact on real-world people. And the economic trends we are currently witnessing are the most dangerous in world history.

But the trail is never obvious. Some of our analysts see things differently. And although you might call that an inconsistency, I believe it is our organization's greatest strength.

We are ignorant of what exact events will befall us tomorrow. We make up for it by allowing many smart people with diverse points of view the opportunity to compete with each other in the marketplace of ideas. This competition is why our network is informally known as "The Agora." *Agora* is the ancient Greek word for marketplace.

By refusing to silence those who disagree with us, we hedge our bets against our own ignorance and allow the very best ideas to rise to the top.

The ideas you are about to receive are ones I have spent an entire career developing and refining. You will find some of them to be common sense. Yet, legions of highly educated people, along with billions of dollars, are being deployed to convince Americans that they are not common sense at all. Others will be less obvious, but no less contested by forces at work in America today.

As a final word before you begin this book, we say again: There are limits to what we know. This is a story with a lot of players, a lot of money flying in a lot of different directions, and a lot of bad ideas.

Many – especially those who are prominent in the media or on Wall Street... or have important positions in the government – have staked their fortunes and their futures on the very system that has brought us to the brink of disaster. They cannot challenge it.

The information you are about to read has never been presented all in one place like this before now. You will not find it in any bookstore or spoken of in any news broadcast.

You are free to make of it what you will, but before you turn this page, I ask that you make yourself a promise...

...That once you turn this page to start reading, you will stick with this book until the very end... And finish what you have started.

It took me 40 years to write it. You can finish this book in mere days... hours even...

As you will see, it is very important that you do.

Sound fair enough?

Then let's begin...

PART 1

In the Ruins of America

CHAPTER 1

Dispatch from an Isolated Mountain Ranch

The light is fading.

The sun has already descended behind one of the many distant mountains that tower over our dry valley here in the mountains of northern Argentina.

As the color drains from the sky, we will begin to lose connection to the outside world as the satellite responsible for our fragile internet connection follows the sun behind the very same mountain.

Suddenly, we will be alone in the universe. Or nearly so…

The brightest stars you have ever seen will fill the cold, thin atmosphere overhead. But any other lights will be solely our own: a mix of greenish solar-powered LED lights and warm, dancing tones from the roaring fire we have just made.

Recently, we got in the 4x4 and drove toward a distant plateau to survey a part of our land we had never before visited.

We kept going up, over rocky trails, pushing further and further outwards from our little edge of civilization. Then we came to a series of lakes. The wind blew hard. There was not a blade of grass anywhere.

Mountain peaks, some snow-covered, surrounded the lakes. Astonishingly, for the place was so inhospitable to life, the lakes were home to thousands of pink flamingos, standing in the shallow water.

"Don't touch the water," one of the locals warned. "It has high levels of arsenic. The arsenic doesn't bother the birds. They must be adapted to it."

What are they doing here? What do they eat? Why are they standing in this freezing, poisonous puddle, hundreds of miles from anything that seems remotely appealing? We wondered.

The guide explained: "There is only one animal in the lake – a tiny form of algae. The flamingos have evolved to come here, wade in the water, and eat it. When they get enough strength and fat on their bodies, they fly away for the winter. They go down to Córdoba in central Argentina. The old ones, though, can't make the flight. They stay all year round."

Silently, we marveled at the fragile chain that had come together to maintain this delicate patch of life... What would happen if the temperature rose just a degree or two? What if the levels of deadly poison suddenly dropped? Could the algae survive without the flamingos and vice versa?

If just one link in that chain were to fail... the poison lake's entire ecosystem might cease to exist, algae and flamingos alike.

Given the odds, this delicate world should have already collapsed into a still and barren world, any trace of what existed long since gone.

Yet, the flamingos return each year. The algae continue to bloom. The ice-cold winds continue to howl.

Confronted with the fragility of the place, the average American do-gooder might gasp in horror. Immediately, he would begin petitioning the White House, posting on Facebook, and desperately looking for something to "occupy."

He would find it unacceptable that such a precarious existence be allowed to exist.

We might point out that the flamingos don't seem to mind. Maybe they like it.

"Well, they're just dumb birds, what do they know?" our do-gooder would respond.

Luckily for the flamingos, improvers, prescriptivists, and do-gooders haven't made it up to the poison lake yet.

They are still hard at work in America, inspecting bathrooms, creating "safe spaces," making sure everyone feels beautiful, and generally failing to mind their own damn business.

Sometimes we are asked why we have a ranch way up here, so far from everything. The land is too dry to support a profitable cattle operation. The place is too far from any fancy restaurants to make selling our wine a sensible idea.

Yes, by most modern standards, being here at the edge of civilization doesn't make much sense at all.

By other standards, however, there is tremendous value in this secluded desert on the margins of the world...

The thin mountain air is not just lacking in O_2, but also refreshingly lacking in bad ideas.

There are no local community meetings on the poison lake issue. There are no op-eds from the *Times* demanding we save the flamingos.

It's not that problems don't abound. We are plagued by drought, isolation, elevation, and lack of just about every service and comfort enjoyed by most of the planet. But with no FEMA, HUD, or even a Waffle House nearby, nature, man, and beast are simply left to sort it out the best they can.

We have no such luxury in the United States.

We have long since given ourselves over to the myth that every problem has a right and just solution: that we can fix that which never asked to be fixed, and improve that which never wanted to be improved.

In other words, we genuinely believe that we can save the flamingos.

And no matter what God, nature, or the flamingos themselves have to say about it, we're going to do just that.

CHAPTER 2

Dead Flamingos

Our thirst to solve, fix, and improve has long been a heady feeding ground for a thousand and one second-rate hustlers, social climbers, and politicians; in other words, men who die rich, respected, and well-sexed.

Take, for instance, the current debate over inequality.

Of great interest to people in America is how much other people earn.

No one – or almost no one – writing in the editorial pages works at McDonald's or earns the minimum wage. But practically every one of the commentators has an opinion about how much people on low wages should earn.

A "living wage" is what they say they want. Thirty-thousand dollars a year is the amount we've seen discussed.

Of course, a national living wage is absurd. It costs far more to live in Manhattan than in the Ozarks. And it is far less expensive to live with Mom and Dad than to have a place of one's own.

But we are not so much concerned with the practical details as with the theory.

We have been told that the people who work at McDonald's need to earn more. But what about those who write for the editorial pages? Perhaps they should earn less?

If well-educated, well-paid columnists can decide the wages of

McDonald's workers, surely the burger flippers should have the right to fix the wages of the chattering, meddling, and improving classes.

Were that to happen, our guess is that the well-paid know-it-alls would take a pay cut. Which seems proper and just.

We walk into McDonald's and a minimum-wage worker serves up our order. We get what we pay for and are content with the transaction; we do not begrudge the worker his recompense.

We read the paper, on the other hand, and we get bilge and nonsense.

Logically, there are only two possibilities when it comes to wages. Either wages are determined by a free give-and-take between those who offer their labor and those who want to buy it. Or someone sets wages according to their own standards.

The do-gooders want to use other people's money to raise the wages of the least well paid, but they make no mention of their own.

Nor do they even offer to pay more for their hamburgers so that McDonald's can pay its workers more.

And what about the poor people who cannot find jobs at all?

If the minimum wage were raised, there would surely be more of them – either because McDonald's could not afford to hire so many people at higher salaries or because it had replaced its minimum-wage employees with machines!

But the price-fixers are so self-satisfied in taking what they think is the high road – driving along comfortably in their Subarus and Priuses – that they can't be bothered to look out the window. If they did, they would see that setting prices always – always! – makes people poorer, not richer.

But it is not only the political and editorial class that fall under the spell of the world improvement myth. It is hard even for the most self-reliant entrepreneur to resist.

Some time ago, Facebook founder Mark Zuckerberg announced that he would give away 99% of his Facebook shares (worth $45 billion at the time) to charity. He was hailed as a model of how the rich should comport themselves.

That kind of money is bound to yield some big payoffs and answer some of the weighty questions facing mankind: Global warming. A cure for cancer. Stopping ISIS. The precise mass of the Higgs boson. Nuclear fusion. Asian fusion.

According to the letter Zuckerberg posted on his Facebook profile after the birth of his daughter, he and his wife are going to focus initially on "personalized learning, internet connectivity, curing disease, and community education."

In the long run, they'll be trying to "advance human potential and promote equality."

Yes, "The Zuck" is on the case... with billions of dollars of do-gooder money. We can feel human potential advancing already, like Hannibal crossing the Alps.

But wait...

How can you advance human potential? How do you know what an "advance" is? How do you know what the "potential" is? How do you know that you are going in the right direction?

Let's look at this gift horse more closely:

Zuckerberg is apparently one of the greatest producers of wealth the world has ever seen. From his Harvard dorm room, he created – from scratch – a social networking site that today is worth $300 billion.

This makes it the seventh most valuable company in the world by market capitalization – even bigger than industrial giant General Electric.

Giving his wealth to charities sounds good. But how is the world a better place when capital is moved from the strong grasp of wealth creators to the limp and slimy hands of the zombies in the nonprofit sector... who have never produced a dime of new wealth?

We don't know.

But the pledge has huge public relations value for Zuckerberg... and for Facebook. And what good is money if it can't buy respect, admiration, and love?

Why bother to buy an expensive watch if you don't want people to admire it... and you?

Why spend millions on fancy home improvements, with a designer kitchen and granite countertops, if it doesn't draw compliments... and perhaps even envy... from the neighbors?

And why give away billions of dollars to charity if it doesn't bring you some favorable press?

Zuckerberg has just paid a huge price to buy the affection and admiration of the public.

You also have to remember the law of diminishing marginal utility... otherwise known as *hormesis*.

The more you have of something, the less each incremental unit is worth to you.

Zuckerberg and his wife have so much money that they can give away 99% of their Facebook shares and still not have to look at the right side of a menu...

...his gift won't force them to take public transportation...

...they won't have to send their daughter to public school or shop at Walmart...

In other words, the money Zuckerberg gives away has near zero real value to him. His lifestyle will be unaffected.

But even if the money isn't particularly important to Zuckerberg, surely it is important to the poor and to humankind? He may be giving it for selfish reasons, but won't it still make the world a better place?

Alas, probably not.

Giving money to strangers on a large scale is rarely a good idea. It makes the giver feel good about themself. But it crushes the givee under the weight of false signals and perverse incentives. (Why bother to plant crops when food is free?)

That is the history of domestic welfare programs, as well as foreign aid: They hurt the people they are supposed to be helping.

Are poor Africans better off after absorbing most of the world's good intentions over the last 100 years?

Apparently not.

Are the people who collect money at stoplights – holding up signs that say they are "homeless veterans" – improved because you flip them a dollar or two?

Maybe not.

Are communities stronger, better, more prosperous, and more virtuous after some rich guy puts his money into the project?

Who knows?

As for making great strides for mankind... you've only made a net gain after you subtracted the net cost.

If a project makes money, it must have produced more than it consumed.

That's why nonprofit activities and charities usually do more harm than good. With no profit motive to guide them, they generally use up more resources than the project deserves.

Managers don't know whether they're going forward or backward. They don't know whether they're adding to the world's wealth and well-being or subtracting from it. They don't know whether they're doing good... or bad.

The trouble is that the world improvers never bother to figure out how the world works.

It is as though they weren't interested. Instead, they just want to control it... to force it in one direction or another... and to mold it, as if it were wet mud.

They ignore the weak voice of common sense emanating faintly from a long-since-atrophied part of their brain that says to leave well enough alone.

We addressed this issue at length in our book, *Hormegeddon*.

There we referenced the work of Joseph Tainter, who explained in his book *The Collapse of Complex Societies* that the decline in civilizations could be traced to problem solving.

Each problem, Tainter says, leads to a solution, which involves greater complexity. Bureaucracies, hierarchies, rules, and regulations are imposed.

With greater complexity comes greater ignorance. You barely know what you are getting into in the first place and your chances of figuring it out actually diminish the more you try.

Of course, no one sings the praises of the presidents, central bankers, or generals who wisely decided to sit on the sidelines.

James Buchanan, who preceded Abraham Lincoln as president, is generally considered America's "worst" president. Why? Because Buchanan decided to leave the irate Southerners alone, suspecting that, over time, cooler heads might prevail. Was he wrong to do so? No one knows, but one thing is certain: There are no monuments to James Buchanan at the National Mall.

CHAPTER 3

Other People's Money

"Señor Bonner," began a fat woman in a colorful sombrero. She wore a dress, but over a pair of pants. Her face was very brown and chubby, with a horizontal mouth lacking several teeth. She has had eight children, we learned later in the conversation.

"The roof of our house fell in. Can you help us repair it?"

Just a few minutes earlier, another woman – similar in build, but with all her teeth and a nice smile – had made her case.

"I have five children. We all sleep in the kitchen of my parents' house. Can you help us build a new house? My parents are tired of having so many children around."

We didn't ask about the children's father. Most of the children in the valley have "unknown" fathers. The older generation – people like our farm manager, Jorge – are scandalized and disgusted.

"It's the government's fault," Jorge explained. "They give money to these girls for each child they have. And if they have seven children, they get a pension.

"When I was growing up, we all worked. We didn't have jobs. We just worked. We thought it was good to work. We planted crops. We took care of animals. We knew that we had to work to survive. We didn't have any money, but at least we didn't depend on government handouts.

"But now the government comes along and tells them that all they need to do is have children... and not get married. So, the young men leave to go to the city and we are left with women having babies. I don't know what is going to happen to this farm."

We don't know, either. But we see what is happening now. Without men in the households, the women turn to the landlord. One asks for a house for her aging mother. Another wants her roof fixed. Another wants a new house for herself and her children. And all these supplications happened within a few minutes. If we had stayed longer, we might have had more.

"What are we going to do?" we asked the farm manager.

"Well, we want to help. But this is a dead end. There is no future in this isolated valley for children. And without fathers. They need to get out into the bigger world... go to school... learn how to do things. We can help all these women to live a little better. But we're not doing them any favors. Because they would be better off moving down to the city."

Welfare makes the giver feel good. But it generally harms the receiver. It makes them dependent. Selfishly, we volunteered to help.

"Maybe we should offer to build a few houses," we suggested.

"You have to learn to tell them 'no,'" Jorge insisted.

"We've seen what happened on other farms. You say 'yes' to one... you've got to say 'yes' to all of them. Then you have a whole community next to the school. And then someone's dog bit someone else... and kids break windows in the school... and things begin to disappear. It's a nightmare."

We've seen this scenario unfold before. Unbeknownst to Jorge, he is describing Baltimore in the 1980s better than even *The Wire* managed. Living in the ghetto during that time, we got to see the effect of government welfare programs firsthand. It was not a pretty sight.

"You get what you pay for," was one of economist Milton Friedman's dicta. You pay people to be poor, unemployed, and in single-mom households – and that's what you get.

And in Baltimore's inner city, we got it good and hard. In the 21217 ZIP code in the early 1980s, there were almost no married couples – other than the few "pioneers" like ourselves who were trying to restore the handsome old buildings.

Almost no one had a real job. And almost no one had any real idea of how the world worked. They thought everybody lived on government handouts; the rich, they thought, just got more handouts than the poor.

It was obvious to us then that welfare programs were a disaster for the people they were supposed to help.

And if not for the fact that those benefitting from them were not the ones paying for them, these programs would have been done away with years ago.

But such is the genius of the modern-day world improvement myth: It is financed entirely with other people's money.

If the money you spend is not your own – and comes to you essentially for free – you have no incentive to stop and ask yourself whether it is being spent wisely.

And that is how we arrive at today's America.

We were lured into a free-money trap by the promise of world improvement.

We got what we paid for.

CHAPTER 4

What We Paid For

There is a natural cycle of boom and bust in the business world. This cycle is helpful because it rids our towns of restaurants with awful food.

Not only does a failed restaurant produce little anxiety, it actually is a source of hope; perhaps a better one will be opened in its place.

Imagine a town with two restaurants. One of them is good. One is marginal.

The marginal one is on the verge of going out of business. Alarmed, the city leaders decide to bail it out.

"We don't want to just have one restaurant," they say. "Think of the jobs that will be lost. We have to do something!"

So, the town's accumulated capital – including money from people who never dine out – is invested in subsidizing the marginal restaurant.

Money interrupts the pattern of boom and bust. One restaurant should have gone bust. Another should have been created. This is merely an illustration of the concept of "creative destruction" developed by Austrian School economist Joseph Schumpeter.

When the boom/bust pattern is halted, there is no punishment for failure... and no reward for innovation. The new restaurant, the one that might have been started by a bright, young entrepreneur with a better idea, never serves a single gluten-free veggie burger.

Creative destruction ceases. The jungle of capitalism is turned into a zoo of cronyism and subsidies. Growth rates decline. Money has not improved lives nor brought forth progress; it has slowed the whole thing down.

The tragedy of modern America is that this phenomenon has gone far beyond the business cycle.

In the Druid Hill area of Baltimore, especially in the summertime, police sirens sang to us every night. Occasionally you'd hear the pop of a pistol, too, followed by the inevitable police car siren. We adapted to it so well; now, we can barely sleep without it.

The black community in Baltimore had adapted, too.

In the labor market, as in all other markets, you compete on price or quality. Young, unskilled black men competed on price. Then, after they learned a skill, they could compete on quality. Minimum wage and Equal Employment Opportunity laws put an end to price competition. Young black men were hit hard. They couldn't get jobs. They couldn't earn money. And they couldn't play their traditional roles in the family.

Families fell apart. And black women turned to government programs – such as food stamps and Aid to Families with Dependent Children – for the support they needed. Housing, medicine, doctor's visits, education, food – it no longer came from the efforts of a coherent family, but from the Great White Welfare System.

Then came the War on Crime in 1965... and the subsequent growth of the prison industry... minimum sentences... helicopters... tanks... and get-tough-on-crime politicians...

After all this, the War on Drugs, circa 1971, did to the Baltimore ghetto what the Royal Air Force did to Dresden.

In the 1980s, we were renovating an old house in a bad neighborhood.

Whenever we could, we hired local teenagers to help. Pookie, Lonzo, and a few others. They were nice and well meaning. But they were completely unskilled... and unreliable.

They had no experience with tools of any sort. Nor had they any concept of punctuality, self-discipline, or forbearance. They had never lived with anyone who had to get up and go to work or save money.

Thanks to the feds' prohibition, profit margins on illegal drugs soared, making the trade irresistible.

By the 1980s, young black men in our neighborhood were almost all involved, or affected, by drugs... and skirmishing regularly for control of important markets.

Inevitably, they did some time in prison. Typically, they were permanently enrolled in the criminal underground before they were out of their teens.

We left the ghetto 20 years ago; it was too dangerous to raise children there. We moved to Europe. Then, years later, we moved back to Baltimore and caught up with friends from the old "hood."

"What happened to the 'boys'?" we asked.

"The ones I kept up with are all dead," said our source. "Murdered... drug overdoses. Pookie was the last of them. Good kid. And smart. His brother was in jail... but he went to community college. We tried to help him by giving him a little remedial tutoring.

"I don't know what happened. But he committed suicide last year."

CHAPTER 5

Ruins

Recently we found ourselves riding out from our *rancho* (ranch house) yet again...

As the sun rose in the sky, it heated the frigid air and we took off our sweaters... also tilting our hats to the north to block the sun.

Our ranch foreman Jorge was mounted on a mule. We were on horses. The mule turned out to be the better choice, because the route we had chosen was only marginally passable.

Several times we had to dismount and urge our horses up and down the steep slopes.

Jorge stayed on his mule and seemed to have no trouble. But our horses often seemed on the verge of disaster, slipping on rocks high above a precipice or skidding on gravel on the ledge of a cliff.

My wife is afraid of heights. She had to avoid looking down to bestill her racing heart.

Your editor had his moments of doubt and fear, too. But he was too busy trying to keep his own footing... or seating... to think much about it.

Before crossing the river, we noticed the telltale signs of ancient habitation. There were abandoned terraces on the hills.

The local people say these were Inca settlements. But they weren't really Incas, according to archaeologists. The Incas were here. But as overlords, not as farmers and settlers.

The Incas had storehouses that were built in a distinctive square style. But the vassal people, who had been here much, much earlier, did the farming.

Whether the people who live in the hills and valleys here today are descended from them or not is a matter of debate. Being labeled "indigenous" comes with a host of entitlements in Argentina, ranging from welfare checks to legally invading land owned by non-Indians.

Thus, many locals claim the heritage of the ancient mountain peoples. However, our friend Sergio explains that this is mostly nonsense: "The Spanish exterminated the Indians that were there in the 16th century."

Still, whatever their fate, they left plenty of traces. Stone terraces show where they lived and farmed. Pottery – with elaborate designs – shows that they were about as advanced technologically as Greece circa 5000 B.C.

Here in America, we have our own traces of a people long gone.

On a hill overlooking the Potomac River, they left a shining Capitol Building.

To the north, on an island between two rivers, they left an Empire State Building that reaches into the clouds.

Down south, they left columned mansions with Spanish moss swaying in the wind.

Out west, they left rows of pumps forever plumbing the depths for oil.

And in graveyards across the country, they left the rusting shells of automobiles that once roared down Main Street, USA.

Americans today dwell among these remnants, living in the ruins of a culture and society that died a long time ago.

Last year, we were fixing up an old farmhouse and needed a new pair of work boots.

To our great delight, we found an old favorite – Red Wing – from an online store. The boots were absurdly expensive – $299 – but we figured we would have them for the rest of our lives.

The boots arrived on Saturday and were just like the ones we bought 40 years ago. Same stiff, solid construction. Same rich smell of leather and last. Same Minnesota simplicity.

But something was different. In with the boots was a magazine celebrating the history of the company. It was a stylish advertising piece; we wouldn't have expected it from such a sweaty, shop-floor boot company.

Even more remarkable were the photos. They showed young people in various chic urban settings: Brooklyn. San Francisco. Berlin. They were all hipsters!

Not a single picture shows a man lifting, toting, turning, hammering, or cutting – the things you're supposed to do in boots like these.

Instead, now they are for hanging out... going to bars... and looking cool. They've become a fashion item.

What happened?

How come America's premier work boots are no longer pitched at America's working men?

One reason: America's working men don't need them...

In 1970, high-quality manufacturing jobs employed 29.5% of America's workers. By 2015, that number had shrunk to 7.7%.

But Red Wing has deeper problems...

First, buyers can get boots cheaper elsewhere. Foreign-made, the new boots are probably just as good and much less expensive.

Second, American workers may not be able to afford American-made work boots.

In real terms, the typical man of working age in the U.S. earns less today than he did in 1975 – 40 years ago.

Also, the "labor participation rate" – which measures the number of people employed or actively looking for work – is back to where it was in 1967.

Back then, it reflected the fact that women were much less likely to have jobs. They stayed at home and looked after families. Now, it's the men who are more likely to be jobless. What they are doing is not clear. But they don't need American-made work boots to do it.

Under the circumstances, Red Wing seems to have made a good move...

Like Harley-Davidson, it has positioned its products as American fashion artifacts – relics of past glories, not modern footwear.

CHAPTER 6

A Nation of "Stable-Fed" Animals

The average citizen is only a few paychecks away from getting put out of his house. He no longer has the freedom to step back... to reflect... to think... to wonder about things... or enjoy the contradictions.

Instead, he must bow before the politicians and financiers who control his livelihood... and place himself at the beck and call of every jackass with a federal ID card.

Consider the stark differences between this man and our Founding Fathers.

Benjamin Franklin "invented" electricity and the Franklin stove. He set up the first public libraries. He was a colorful writer... a self-made man... an accomplished diplomat.

Thomas Jefferson introduced Palladian architecture to the colonies. He founded the University of Virginia and designed its campus. He wrote and spoke several European languages, studied Native American culture and languages, and created his own version of the Bible.

He was a scholar, a statesman, the author of the Declaration of Independence, a scientist... the list goes on and on.

Thomas Jefferson... Benjamin Franklin... George Washington – would any of them recognize in the United States of America any trace of the country they tried to establish?

Washington warned against "foreign entanglements." But now the U.S. is tangled up all over the world.

Jefferson charged that British King George III had "sent forth a swarm of agents to harass the people and eat out their substance." But the tax rate then was less than 5%. Today, for residents of California or Maryland, it is about 50%.

Then, the "swarm" of agents was so thin on the ground that an American – especially one on the frontier – might live his entire life without ever meeting an employee of His Majesty's government.

Today, he can hardly go a single day without running into a bureaucrat who is giving him orders:

"Take off your shoes... put your laptops, tablets, and smartphones on the belt... You must fill out this 1022-X form... You must have a permit... You could face a fine of up to $10,000 and six months in jail..."

The typical American of today can't afford freedom or courage. He hasn't time or money for them.

He has been turned into what economist Wilhelm Röpke called a "stable-fed" animal, dependent on his masters.

His masters offer him two options: Either take on debt he can't afford or take property from someone else.

There is a third option, self-reliance, but the risks it entails appear loathsome to most.

Imagine the courage and the spirit required to load your family and property into a rickety covered wagon and set out across the wastelands of Dakota, the jagged peaks of Utah, and deathly valleys of California... with nothing but God and a wide, forbidding horizon as your keepers.

Today, millennials from air-conditioned homes who grew up with computers and never lacked for food to eat take to the streets demanding free college... a guaranteed basic income... and subsidized rent.

Stable-fed animals, indeed.

CHAPTER 7

Cutting in Line

Thus, at some point over the past 200 years, we went from being a people on the move to a people on the take.

And despite its pretensions of egalitarianism, not all have benefitted equally from this new arrangement... In fact, a growing number of Americans seem to have suddenly realized that this new system of modern serfdom is not to their benefit at all...

The following allegory – or "deep story," as she calls it – is taken from author and professor Arlie Hochschild. We reproduce it with some edits (in italics) of our own:

> You are patiently standing in the middle of a long line stretching toward the horizon, where the American Dream awaits. But as you wait, you see people cutting in line ahead of you. *These line-cutters are members of what the government calls "protected" and "disadvantaged" groups – beneficiaries of a thousand federal aid programs.* As you wait in this unmoving line, you're being asked to feel sorry for them all. You have a good heart. But who is deciding who you should feel compassion for? Then you see *celebrities and politicians* waving the line-cutters forward. *They're on the line-cutters' side.* As you wait your turn, *they're* using the money in your pocket to help the line-cutters. *Their elitist* backers have removed the shame from taking. The government has become an instrument for redistributing your money to the undeserving. It's not your government anymore; it's theirs.

Hochschild would likely tell you that the above allegory is just a story, not really how America works.

But her allegory has more truth to it than she cares to admit.

There is no conspiracy to keep the white middle class down. There is no conspiracy to rid the world of men, or conservatives, or even liberty itself.

But there is a corruption in our national and collective character.

And that corruption has very real effects on everyday life.

What happens when you give preferential treatment – under the law – to certain groups over others is that the value of belonging to specific groups increases.

And soon enough, the rational citizen sees that he is better off belonging to one of those specific groups than trying to get by on his own.

Which is easier for the prospective college applicant:

To get by on grades, extracurricular activities, and personality alone to set you apart from the hordes of other, similar applicants?

Or to claim a Cherokee, African, or even Alaskan Native heritage?

But careful of which one you choose! The ins and outs of identity and entitlement grow more complex by the day.

For example, Asians may be a minority in the United States, but their success in educational achievement, business, and building strong communities has come at a cost.

Ivy League colleges have now been accused of a sort of reverse discrimination against Asians.

It doesn't pay to reach too high.

Such a corruption is the necessary effect of the constant give and take from one group to another... of the continuous failures in world improvement... of the endless promotion of a Hobson's choice between entitlement or alienation...

But sadly, it is not the worst consequence of these things.

The worst consequence is that the social bonds between us grow increasingly brittle, and the nation as a whole begins to irreparably weaken.

The working-class man in Louisiana used to have a decent wage and could expect a pension upon retirement. Now his job has been shipped overseas, his social security is taxed, his healthcare is through the roof, and to top it all off, he is now being told that he is somehow a child of privilege... that no one in Washington... no one on Wall Street... no one at the United Nations... will be fighting for him. In fact, they'll be fighting against him.

What is he to do except resent the African-American man of the inner city who seems to be rolling in government aid?

On the other side, when African-American communities vote promisors of a new dawn, only to wake up to the same old morning the next day, is it any wonder our inner cities burn as they have in Baltimore, Ferguson, Charlotte, New York, Los Angeles, and Detroit?

When the reward for working hard to build a business is the jackboot of regulation and taxation on your throat, is it any wonder that our best and brightest are defecting elsewhere at increasingly alarming rates?

From 1999 to 2014, the number of people leaving the U.S. to live elsewhere more than doubled.

When you can make more money collecting disability than working a job (with a prescription for powerful pain pills as the cherry on top), is it any wonder that entire towns in West Virginia seem to be "disabled"?

Is it any wonder that heroin overdoses – a cheaper high than prescription pain pills – are now skyrocketing among otherwise normal young people?

Today the citizenry casts about desperately for a group to blame, be it the Republicans, the Democrats, the "privileged whites," the "unwed mothers," the "illegal immigrants," the "greedy rich," the "lazy poor"...

But few understand that our current predicament was nurtured into being by a different group altogether – one mostly unseen and undocumented...

And that the true origins of our fragile society are not social or even cultural.

They are economic.

In the next part of this book, we will examine the little-known shift in our economic structure that perverted our nation...

What follows will detail how that structure must break, suddenly and irreparably.

In the second half of this book, you will learn about various strategies, ideas, and methods for dealing with such a collapse.

You may not be able to act on all of them. We don't necessarily recommend you do. Everyone is different. Yet, it is our hope that you walk away from this book with enough understanding to not be caught off guard, and the tools to be prepared if you so choose.

With that we leave you for now... Soon, the Southern Cross – a constellation only seen in the Southern Hemisphere – will appear in the sky above us. The chill in the air tells us it is time to move inside, start a fire, and open a bottle of Malbec.

The gauchos are coming in from the pastures. The cattle are huddling together for the night.

Here at the ranch, nature itself has signed off. So must we.

PART 2

The Great Lie

CHAPTER 8

Something Went Wrong on the Way to the Future

Today's economy no longer seems to work for the average American.

His earnings go down. His debt goes up. He works longer to stay in the same place.

He had to work 990 hours to buy a Ford F-150 pickup in 1976. Forty years later, he has to put in 1,220 hours.

The Census Bureau has the average American working man's income, in 2012 dollars, at about $37,000 in 1972 – its highest level of the decade. Today, it is close to $34,000.

We suspect that, using different numbers, we might find an even more severe drop. But the remarkable thing is that we are doing this calculation at all. We shouldn't be wondering about it. It should be obvious that we are all far better off today than we were a half-century ago.

This should have been the easiest period in human history in which to make financial progress.

Never before have there been so many inventors and entrepreneurs. Never before have they had so much accumulated science and capital to work with.

Never before have there been so many people making things... and so many consumers with money in their pockets to buy them.

And never before were there so many earnest lawmakers, Ph.D. economists, curious researchers, diligent policymakers, and nonprofit-employed do-gooders – millions of people all doing their level best to make us happier, healthier, and richer!

Something seems to have gone wrong on the way to the future.

Clipping Coins

We begin with two principles:

1. Money is not wealth.

2. Government cannot create wealth.

Although government can conjure up millions, billions, even trillions of "new" dollars out of thin air – thus, creating more *money* – it cannot create more *wealth*.

Normally, money is just a way of keeping track of wealth. It's like a clock. You can't slow down your clock to claim that the day is longer. That's because a clock isn't the same as time; it just measures it. In the same way, you can't print excess money and claim you have produced more wealth.

Thus, money is not wealth. The best money can pretend to be is a representation of earned wealth.

The trouble is that, over time, money and wealth tend to diverge.

Even in the days of gold coins, thieves would clip and shave their edges, keeping the little extra gold for themselves before passing the now-devalued coins off to some unsuspecting mark. The recipient of these coins would have the same amount of *money*, but less *wealth*.

Similarly, those manning the printing presses today always have an incentive to enrich themselves by printing just a few more precious dollars for their own use.

Although the process is different, the effect of money printing is the same as that of coin clipping. Because each new paper bill dilutes the value of money already in existence, the holders of those dollars are suddenly poorer – even though they have the same amount of money they had before. In effect, the money printer has extended an invisible hand into another's vault and clipped his coins.

By his actions, the money printer is ensuring that money and wealth become more and more estranged, until the two barely recognize each other.

When that happens, you get inflation. And not the kind you can cure with Tums and a glass of water.

We've all heard the campfire tales of the dreaded hyperinflationary crisis: people going to the groceries with wheelbarrows full of cash… using worthless cash as wallpaper.

These stories are good for a thrill but fail to reflect the far more mundane – and terrifying – aspect of hyperinflation: It steals time.

Did you spend your entire career working hard to put a little money aside? Looking forward to retiring, never paying another dime in income tax, and living off the fruits of your labors?

Hyperinflation resets the clock, putting you right back into the same financial position as when you were just starting out… as if the last 40 years of work had never even happened at all.

Except that you're not actually younger… and you can't go back and start all over again.

In essence, the harder you work, the poorer you get. You have expended a key resource: time. You have received nothing – or at least an insufficient amount – in return.

So you can't just print money and call it wealth… Nor can government create wealth. It can only print money.

Fortunately for our rulers, this bedrock law of monetary physics is easily forgotten when the right amount of Ivy League education is paired with a sincere desire to fleece the common man for everything he's got.

And forgotten it was at some point between August 13th and 15th in the year 1971, when President Nixon and 15 advisers were holed up at Camp David.

CHAPTER 9

In the Beginning

The U.S. government had, since the days of Washington, minted coins – called dollars – containing a certain amount of gold or silver. However, these early dollars had two principal drawbacks.

First, their value could not be changed on a whim. Were the feds to try, people could simply melt down the coins for their gold content.

Second, no one was forced to use the coins. The states and various private banks issued their own currency. If the good people of Virginia, for example, felt uneasy about an overly indebted central government controlling their money, they could simply switch to local Virginia currency and tell the government to go suck wind.

The result, of course, was that the federal government was told to go do that quite a lot and began to develop a bit of a complex about it.

To solve those twin problems, Congress passed a series of laws, culminating in the National Banking Acts of 1863 and 1864, which created a network of nationally chartered banks and taxed state currency out of existence.

The "Legal Tender Note" (as the U.S. dollar was called) became America's sole currency.

Having triumphed over its competition in the money market, the federal government next took aim at the banking system itself. What it found especially galling about the banking sector was that banks ultimately answered not to the District of Columbia, but to their customers. If they fooled around with client money, and the clients found out, the banks could be obliterated by withdrawal demands.

The idea that the common man could ruin such reputable members of society as bankers no doubt kept elected officials waking in cold sweat.

A series of such bank runs in 1907 gave them a golden opportunity to convince the public that they had better intervene. In response, they passed the Federal Reserve Act of 1913, creating a central authority which would keep the banks afloat in case their clients sought to ruin them.

But the Act did more than just establish total control over the banking sector.

It also sought to create an "elastic currency."

And that, dear reader, is where our troubles begin.

CHAPTER 10

A New Money in America

What is an elastic currency and why would government want one?

"Elastic currency" is simply banking jargon for printing more money.

In effect, the Federal Reserve was charged with diluting the value of existing dollars by printing new ones.

The results that followed were predictably terrible. The dollar lost 93% of its value.

Purchasing Power of One U.S. Dollar (1913 - Present)

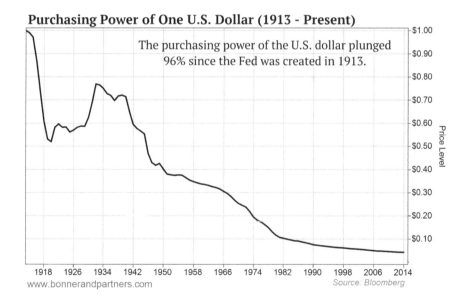

But the benefits to the insiders who created this elastic money were many.

First, the government debt became easier to pay off.

Second, they found a way to artificially create economic stimulus.

As an economy gets wealthier, each dollar – meant to track the amount of wealth in a society – becomes more valuable. Each holder of a dollar becomes a kind of investor in the overall growth and health of the economy. No need for piddling interest from a savings account; your cash dollars can grow in value without any bank at all.

Inevitably, as each dollar represents more wealth, the person holding that dollar will become more and more careful about spending it. As people save instead of buying more junk they don't need, the economy undergoes a natural cooling phase, before once again entering a heating phase when people are finally ready to spend a little.

Now imagine you're a politician up for re-election during a cooling phase. New jobs aren't springing up at quite the rate they were before. Everyone's a little leaner.

Do you:

a. Remember the wisdom of Joseph from the Book of Genesis, encourage people to save, and reassure them that it won't last but a few years?

b. Find a way to artificially inflate the economy by forcing people to spend their hard-saved dollars?

In 1913, the federal government opted for Option B.

And they've been hard at work fulfilling that mandate ever since.

At the time, it must have seemed like the greatest world improvement of all time. The feds found a way to defeat the natural economic cycle, or so it appeared.

What they refused to take into account, no doubt leaving it for the next guy to worry about, is that over a long enough timeline, Mother Nature always wins.

Cue the Great Depression... In the 1930s, economists working for the Roosevelt administration managed to stretch out a depression over an entire decade (they had previously only lasted a few months).

Did they take the hint?

No, the world improvers, right-thinkers, and politicos of the world went right on patting each other on the back, blaming the other side, and eventually got so busy fighting wars that they forgot about a time before economic manipulation altogether.

Of course, in the early days at least, there was a limit on the manipulation in which they might engage.

And no, it wasn't common decency. It was gold.

If you'll recall, up until the 1970s, the U.S. dollar was known as the "Legal Tender Note." If that sounds more like a legal contract than a form of money, it is for good reason. Each "Legal Tender Note" could be redeemed for a set amount of gold at the so-called "gold window" of the Federal Reserve.

What's so great about gold?

Well, the yellow metal has no magic properties. It is simply the case that gold must be dug out of the ground with much effort and stored. On top of that, gold becomes harder and harder to get as time goes on. You have to dig deeper each time.

Just as wealth is created with time and effort, so too is gold.

In other words, gold is just money, but it is money tethered, inexorably, to wealth.

By allowing citizens to redeem their U.S. dollars in gold, the value of our money could not diverge terribly far from wealth. And the U.S. government was limited in how much new money it could flood into the system.

That all came to an end in 1971.

On August 15th of that year, President Nixon went before the nation to announce that the U.S. dollar was no longer convertible into gold.

(To be fair to Mr. Nixon, he was not the first to knock gold from its throne. That was President Johnson's doing, with the passage of the Gold Reserve Requirement Elimination Act of 1968...)

Thus, our money became disconnected from wealth.

And once the link was severed, neither Nixon, nor almost anyone else, had a clear idea of what the new monetary era really meant.

Only now are we beginning to understand how this new money corrupted the country and undermined its wealth.

Because what happened after 1971 went much further than inflation and money printing.

CHAPTER 11

What Went Wrong
at the Turn of the Century

Let's go back to the politician up for re-election. He has attempted to conquer the natural economic cycle by detaching the dollar from gold, allowing him a truly "elastic" money that he can print at will to stimulate the U.S. economy.

Eventually, however, the stimulation stops being so stimulating (an example of diminishing returns, or *hormesis*, as we noted at the beginning of this book). Our politician knows that at some point, if he prints too much, the value of the dollar will begin to drop so fast that it will cause an economic disaster of its own.

But re-election is coming. And he has already ruined his constituents with giveaways to various special interests, entitlements, and bad economics. Now they are broke, jobless, and the pitchforks are coming out if he doesn't think of something fast.

His solution is ingenious, if dastardly and short-sighted.

He floods the economy with debt.

Under the gold-backed money system, the ratio of debt to GDP was fairly constant.

Until the 1970s, it was about 1.5-to-1.

More than anything else, this signaled the abiding connection between the dollar, debt, and real economic output. You couldn't lend what you didn't have. And you couldn't have it if you didn't earn it (GDP). But take away the gold, as the feds did in 1968 and 1971, and you take away the limit. Credit could run wild.

Now, the ratio of credit to GDP is about 3.2-to-1. For every dollar of real GDP output, in other words, there are more than three dollars of debt.

That represents about $35 trillion of unfinished transactions – borrowing and buying (but not repaying) – over the last 40 years that shouldn't have happened.

You can see it all over America... the houses, shopping malls, corporate debt, golf courses, wars, prisons, bonuses, credit card bills, mortgages, apartments, and cruise lines – $35 trillion worth of things that wouldn't exist had it not been for the Fed's credit money.

 In the wake of 1971, credit began replacing real money in our economy at a rate never before seen.

Every time our economy slowed, government and banking officials simply injected more credit – like a shot of adrenaline to the heart.

But what they've been keeping alive is not the real economy. It is a fantasy, like a man with zero equity in the house he says he owns.

This fantasy economy has distorted and damaged our entire society... our economy, our government... even our families.

Just look around.

Malls where people shop on credit. Houses bought on credit, never actually owned... always refinanced. Cars financed for 84 months at 0% interest. Meals consumed in fast food restaurants, paid for with credit. Students in college... only because credit makes it easier to go to university than to find a decent job.

And no wonder. The decent jobs – the "breadwinner" jobs – are hard to find. Only 50% of working-age people have full-time jobs. And only half earn more than $30,000 a year.

Why?

Because the cheap credit system made it easy to move the good jobs somewhere else... and made it hard to create better jobs at home.

New jobs come with new businesses. But the percentage of businesses less than a year old... and the percentage of the workforce that works for them... are only about half of what they were in 1980.

In the old days, business startups would be financed from savings – often from friends and families.

But today, who's got savings? Who needs them when you've got unlimited credit on tap?

And as the breadwinner jobs went, so went the breadwinners. In post-1970s households, husband and wife won the bread. Families needed two paychecks, not just one.

You may ask, "What's the problem? People decided for themselves... Women preferred to work."

Yes, but they didn't decide in a vacuum. They decided in the wind tunnel of flying credit... and soaring prices. Salaries stagnated in the '70s. What were women to do?

Today, you can get any food you want at the supermarket – already prepared for you. Or you can go out to any one of dozens of different fast-food or family eateries. All very convenient.

You may say, "Well, consumers have spoken. That's what they want." But with husband and wife working, what choice did they have?

They got the convenience of eating out. But they gave up something that economists couldn't measure – the pleasure of preparing and eating home-cooked meals... the stability of having someone who was at home and focused on the family full-time... someone who was not part of the credit-fueled, work-a-day economy.

The quality of family life changed. For the better? Hard to say.

Fast food restaurant income went up. GDP went up. More burger-flippers were hired. Economists looked upon their work like God gazing at the world he had just created.

"It was good," they said. "The greatest world improvement of them all."

In fact, it is the greatest lie in American history.

And I can prove it.

CHAPTER 12

The Great Lie

Lately, it seems that knowledge itself has become corrupted.

According to official numbers provided by the World Bank, U.S. GDP rose from 1989 to 2015 by about 12.3 trillion dollars. But are those numbers really any good?

We asked our expert researcher Nick Rokke to do a bit of recalculating.

"What if you figured out the inflation rate the way the government did under the Reagan administration?" we asked.

"And what if you adjusted today's GDP for a more honest rate of inflation?"

"Wow!" says Nick. "You'd get a 'real' (inflation-adjusted) GDP *loss* of 60% since 1989."

Wow is right... All the growth of the last 27 years disappears. Instead, we've been living through a massive depression.

Of course, we use our numbers; other economists use theirs. And the truth is probably somewhere in the middle.

But ask any person who has or is currently working for a living and they will no doubt see more than a hint of truth in our recalculation.

The feds' numbers might not show it, but a lot of people in America – especially in "flyover America" – live it. They have less real income than they had in the '70s. And higher costs. Medical care, for example, now costs nearly 10 times what it did when Ronald Reagan entered the White House.

Today, that reality is finally starting to settle in. The citizenry now finds itself living in a strange sort of serfdom... in someone else's house. On someone else's money. Often driving in someone else's automobile. And sometimes even sitting on someone else's furniture.

Got a health problem? Oh, yes – check into someone else's health system. Want an evening out at a restaurant? Put it on a credit card; let someone else pay for it.

Serfs don't necessarily live poorly; they live badly. Because they're not in control of the resources they need to live well. They are dependent, not independent.

As dependents, their minds, their morals, and eventually their very bodies start to atrophy and decline.

A recent paper by economics Nobel Prize winner Angus Deaton and his co-author Anne Case highlights a very disturbing trend – death rates are increasing for white people in America, especially for working-class middle-aged whites. The increase looks like it has been going on since the late 1990s.

For white Americans with no college education, deaths have soared. Other groups of men – Hispanic and black – live longer. Why would life expectancy be going in the opposite direction for whites? The proximate causes, according to the Deaton-Case paper, were drugs, alcohol, and suicide. But what's behind it... and why?

In 1965, Daniel Patrick Moynihan's famous report on the "Negro Family" warned that black families were being destroyed. Out-of-wedlock babies, family breakups, poverty, drugs, violence, unemployment, prison – blacks were actually falling further and further behind whites, he noted.

But now it is poor or "middle-class" whites who are being left for dead. Why?

We'll take a guess: As the breadwinner jobs disappeared, white men lost their sense of purpose and place. Men could no longer "bring home the bacon"; women had less use for them. When women have no use for men, men soon get up to mischief.

Of course, this trend will not last forever.

Because we are now nearing the end of this era in the American story.

If you'll recall, up until the 1970s, a dollar of debt produced at least a dollar of GDP growth. Credit was a powerful investment.

But as it goes with all things, eventually we start to see diminishing returns in its power to keep the debt economy running.

Nowadays, it costs $10 of debt to produce a single-dollar rise in the GDP. The system is going bad.

Soon, the credit-for-growth machine must break down altogether.

PART 3

The Great American Credit Collapse

CHAPTER 13

Cash Will Disappear

We begin with a letter from a *Bill Bonner Letter* subscriber:

> Bill: I just finished your book *Hormegeddon* and I am a
> recent subscriber to your newsletter. I agree with all of your
> predictions and everything you're saying. What is the best way
> to position yourself to profit and protect yourself from the
> upcoming collapse we all know is coming?

I didn't intend to answer the question.

But I found I had a few ideas...

First, though, I will take a crack at trying to picture the
circumstances... the events that will lead to the calamity we need
protection from.

This is a calamity that your correspondent has seen coming for so
long, he's beginning to feel he may be doing you a disservice by
warning you. Like a podiatric surgeon who botched an operation, he
looks at the dead patient and feels it is time to brush up on anatomy.
Maybe the foot bone is not connected to the ankle bone after all.

The trouble is, the textbooks are written by people whose view of
economic anatomy is mechanistic, not humanistic. They have fixes
for every problem and wrenches in both hands.

Yes, we could go back to earlier tomes – by the great economists
Bastiat, Say, Schumpeter, von Mises, and Hayek. There, we'd find
the old-time religion... the real flesh and blood of real economics...
with crime and punishment, sin and retribution, heavy hammers
and swollen thumbs. But they lived in a different world... at least,

that is what their critics tell us... before central bankers walked on water.

Instead, we try to look far ahead, to where we might be going.

For dramatic tension, let's explore what it might look like to the average unprepared American. Come with me. Not into *the* future, for we can't know what the future will be. But into *a* future.

"Temporarily Out of Service"

One day you will feel a horrible, sick fear, deep in your stomach... and a hot sweat on the back of your neck...

You will be suddenly, deeply upset with yourself.

You knew there was something wrong with "the system"... You knew that at some level it just didn't make sense; you knew it couldn't go on like that forever. You knew you should have done something to protect yourself. You knew it all had to come to an end somehow... sometime.

But it was always "too early" to make a big change. And now it is too late.

Everything seemed so normal for so long... you went along with everyone else... trusting... hoping it would all turn out all right. You didn't want to look like an alarmist... or a nut.

And now, standing in front of your ATM, you will be on the brink of panic. Because you have exactly $29 in your wallet. You need more cash. This is the third machine you've gone to. All say the same thing: "Temporarily Out of Service."

You knew the situation was spinning out of control. But the machines worked two days ago. Yes, they were already limiting the amount you could take out to just $200. Still, they worked. Why would they stop now?

And now, you need them more than ever. Everyone does.

This "financial crisis" is strange. Nobody wants cash... but everybody needs it! Cash is losing its value – fast. But how else can you buy things... and pay your bills?

There's been some talk in Congress of forcing stores to accept credit cards and checks... But you've tried the Food Lion. "Credit Cards Not Accepted..."

You've tried the Whole Foods. Same story. "Cash Only." And the cash machine has a sign on it: "Out of Order." Someone has scrawled on it: "BS."

You get back in your car. But you are down to an eighth of a tank. The gas stations stopped taking credit cards yesterday. They only take cash. Because they can take the cash out at the end of the day to one of the "money changers" who operate out of vans in mall parking lots. They suddenly appeared a few weeks ago. Now, they're everywhere.

You are getting desperate. You have food in the house for about 24 hours. Maximum. You need to buy more. But how can you buy anything without money?

You thought you were sitting pretty, financially speaking. After the third big crash, the government came up with the "QE for the People" program. And now your stocks are higher than ever.

But you don't have any money! Yes, you could sell your stocks. You could get a check. Who will cash it? Well, the guy at the money-changer van will... for a BIG discount.

Still, there are long lines at the "money changers." Some people are desperate to get cash. Others are desperate to get rid of it. Really, desperation is what the whole thing is about. Everybody is desperate.

The "money changers" work like pawnshops... or outlaw banks. You take your rings and other jewelry. They trade them for cash on the spot. Or, if you have cash... you take it there and buy whatever you think will hold its value. Merchants don't take their cash to the banks; they don't want to run afoul of the "anti-speculating" rules. So they take them to these money changers and get valuables in return.

And of course, the money changers are getting rich. Which people don't like very much. There are reports that some have been arrested by the police. Some have been robbed. At least a couple of them have been murdered.

The whole country is jittery... and scared... Strange things are beginning to happen.

And now this. You will have to go get some of your wife's jewelry and get in line. You know they'll give you only a fraction of what it is really worth. That's why you didn't do it before. You knew it was a rip-off.

So, you hesitated... because you thought the problem would be fixed. Instead, it got worse.

What's Anything Worth? Who Knows?

Who could have imagined a Dow at 50,000? You didn't... but it recently shot past 100,000. Yes, some guys are making a fortune in stocks... and in real estate.

The house down the block... it sold for $350,000 in 2014. Last week, someone paid $1.5 million... You thought he was crazy. But now, you're not so sure. It's beginning to look like a smart move.

The last time you filled your tank, gasoline cost you $20 a gallon. A Happy Meal at McDonald's was $19. If this keeps up, that $1.5 million house could seem like a bargain.

All this happened so fast. In just a couple of months, everything that you thought was stable... and solid... It all turned to mush and muck. You've got both feet on the ground, but the ground gives way. What happened?

But there's no time to think this through now. You barely have enough gas to drive home... let alone drive back to a money changer with your wife's jewelry.

What are you going to do?

What are others doing?

That's the trouble. There are about 300 million other people – in about the same boat. Everyone needs cash...

They need dollars to pay for gas. They need dollars to pay for food. They need dollars to pay for all the things we take for granted.

If you had the gas, maybe you could drive to another ATM... or even another city... or go directly into the bank and ask for cash. But the banks have been closed because of the "emergency." And according to your car radio, it is worse in other places:

> *Crowds of people broke into convenience stores in two Detroit neighborhoods this morning. Police report a wave of similar robberies in several cities. In at least one incident, robbers left credit cards with a note: "Charge my account... I didn't have a choice."*

In Baltimore, Maryland, police were out in force throughout the downtown area. The mayor told reporters that "snatch-and-run crime has become an epidemic." Most often stolen are food items from local convenience stores. One man was shot dead at Mondawmin Mall. Police believe the man was engaged in money changing.

If everyone needs cash, why won't the government just print more? It will. But it takes time. News reports will tell you the government is preparing emergency dollars that will be distributed through the banks.

But what is this new money worth?

No Exceptions

What's happening back here in the present that would cause that kind of breakdown?

What is going wrong?

In a nutshell, America does not run on cash. It runs on credit. In theory, America's line of credit is unlimited... but in practice... it can get complicated, fast.

The U.S. is the first and largest economy ever to function on credit.

Americans have 3.75 credit cards per person. They do some 60 million credit card transactions every day: 67% of gasoline purchases are done with credit cards, 62% of travel expenses, 67% of clothing. About 40% of low- and middle-income households use them to pay basic living expenses – rent, mortgage, groceries, and utilities. And more and more shopping is done online – 100% of it with some form of plastic.

Today, less than a third of all commercial transactions are settled in cash. The rest are on credit. **When the credit cards stop working, the economy stops.**

Listen closely to your car radio after the crisis begins:

> *The financial crisis took a turn for the worse today. Governor Christie of New Jersey and Governor Brown of California announced emergency measures to force gas stations to continue accepting credit cards. But commuters in northern New Jersey as well as Southern California found local gas stations closed this morning. Whether they closed to avoid having to accept credit cards... or whether they actually have no more gas has not been established.*

> *Our news helicopters reported many abandoned vehicles along commuter highways. Apparently, drivers simply ran out of gas.*

When a money system breaks down, everything breaks down.

Again, let's listen to the radio of the future:

> *Las Vegas receives almost all of its food deliveries by truck and the truckers say they don't have the cash to pay for fuel. California governor Brown had ordered the gas stations to accept credit cards, but the stations say they don't have the fuel to sell.*

> *With food deliveries slowed... and in some places, stopped altogether... shelves of many grocery stores are bare. For the moment, it's calm here. Emergency supplies – usually made available only in the event of a natural disaster – are making their way to Las Vegas neighborhoods. But those will soon be depleted.*

> *The financial shock seems to have reached far beyond Las Vegas. Reports coming into the newsroom tell us of desperate people all over the country... food riots have broken out in several places. And in Denver, what can only be described as a "money riot" left two men dead, after a crowd stormed a money changer's van and overturned it.*

The worst thing is that the chain of supply that fills shops, supermarkets, and gas stations seems to have come to a stop. Experts say the gas stations are running out of fuel because they can't settle their accounts. That is, they can't buy more fuel because they don't have the money to buy it. And the truckers don't have the money to buy the gas even if the gas stations had any. It looks like the whole system is breaking down.

If this continues for more than a few days, we could be seeing some serious problems... the economy seems to be coming to a halt. And people need food.

Is this over-the-top paranoia? Is my doom and gloom out of control? I hope so. Maybe it won't happen. Maybe it won't be so bad. But history shows that financial catastrophes do happen.

No one wants them. No one plans them. But no one can stop them. Every credit expansion ends in a credit contraction. No exceptions.

Then, how will the biggest credit expansion in history end?

CHAPTER 14

When the Money Goes Bad

Approximately $1.5 trillion changes hands – not including investments – in the U.S. every month. People buy milk and pay babysitters. They pay their mortgages and their taxes. Consumer spending alone is $11.2 trillion annually.

But as of 2015, there is only $1.2 trillion worth of dollars – physical money – in the entire world. Approximately 50%-75% of that is overseas. And much of the stock of dollars is "dead money" – stuffed in mattresses, safe deposit boxes, and so forth. (Don't worry; it will come alive when the credit bubble bursts – and wreak more havoc.)

Credit is what makes the wheels turn. Without it, almost everything comes to a halt. The banks... the gas stations... the grocery and convenience stores, too. The delivery trucks stop, and we are all in very big trouble...

Credit depends on stable money. One person lends to another, expecting that what they'll get back will be worth roughly what they lent out. When the value of money begins to change rapidly, folks stop lending.

Impossible? Unlikely? Not going to happen? Well, as you can see in the following table, it's already happened in other countries.

Something similar has been happening in Venezuela since 2014. Inflation will soon top 1,600% according to *The Wall Street Journal*. At one point, speculators were giving the country a 91% chance of defaulting.

I'm intrigued... But I've been discouraged from visiting by the instinct of self-preservation. According to the U.S. embassy, foreigners – especially obvious gringos like me – are targeted for robbery and kidnapping.

Country	Dates	Peak Rate of Inflation
Chile	1973	88%
Hungary	1923-1924	98%
Peru	1988	114%
Zaire	1991-1992	114%
Azerbaijan	1991-1994	118%
Uzbekistan	1992	118%
Bulgaria	1997	123%
Austria	1921-1922	129%
Kazakhstan	1992	141%
Kyrgystan	1992	157%
Belarus	1992	159%
Bolivia	1984-1985	183%
Argentina	1989-1990	197%
Georgia	1992	198%
Tajikistan	1992-1993	201%
Georgia	1993-1994	211%
Soviet Union	1922-1924	212%
Soviet Union	1992	245%
Zaire	1993-1994	250%
Nicaragua	1986-1991	261%
Poland	1923-1924	275%
Ukraine	1992-1994	285%
China	1943-1945	302%
France	1795-1796	304%
Bosnia/Herzegovina	1992-1993	322%
Peru	1990	397%
Taiwan	1945	399%
Taiwan	1948-1949	399%
Turkmenistan	1992-1993	429%
Armenia	1993-1994	438%
Free City of Danzig	1922-1923	2,437%
China	1947-1949	5,070%
Germany	1922-1923	29,525%
Greece	1941-1945	138,000%
Republika Srpska	1992-1994	297 million %
Zimbabwe	2007-2008	8 billion %
Yugoslavia	1992-1994	313 billion %
Hungary	1945-1946	41.6 quadrillion %

Apparently, the criminals think nothing of killing you, as they did the former Miss Venezuela, if they think that makes their business transaction easier.

I am fully dedicated to providing you with the best information and commentary on the market, dear reader, but there are limits. We'll have to rely on published reports.

Here is one. The *Financial Times*, December 2, 2014:

> We are beggars of food, beggars of basic products, beggars of medicines, beggars of diapers for our children – right now we are beggars of everything... Inflation eats us up; we have hit rock bottom. We cannot get any worse.

The person from whose lips these words came was standing in line in Caracas to buy food. A long line. And when she finally got to the counter, she found her options had been reduced. When the money goes bad, the whole economy goes bad. Prices go crazy. Government reacts with controls. The shelves empty. The economy sinks. But you're probably thinking... Oh, the U.S. is nothing like those countries... it can't happen here.

And you're right. It won't be much like any of those financial disasters. It could be worse. Much worse.

Why the Cash Disappears

All of the credit crises listed above might have been small potatoes... just a rehearsal for the big implosion of debt and credit that lies ahead.

Yes, financial chaos in Zimbabwe and Argentina and elsewhere was bad. People lost their savings. Some lost their homes and their retirements. Some even lost their lives.

But those foreign disasters were nothing compared to the one coming right here in the U.S. Why?

First, this one is much, much bigger. The Argentine economy was only $610.3 billion – about the size of Chicago's metropolitan area. Its total outstanding credit in 2000 was only $132 billion. Compare that to the U.S. with a GDP of $17 trillion and a total credit market debt of $12.6 trillion (all as of December 2014).

Second, this one is much, much wider, too. Almost every modern economy is implicated. All have similar problems. All are reacting in similar – and similarly ineffective – ways. And, as of the end of 2014, the total debt worldwide is now more than $200 trillion. In 1980, before the big run-up in credit began, the total was just $900 billion.

Third, those are just numbers. The crucial thing to remember is that none of those countries depended on credit the way we do in the U.S. The Argentines and the Zimbabweans, for example, didn't have many credit cards... or mortgages... or ATMs... or automatic gasoline pumps.

In Venezuela, at the time of writing, a few credit cards are still being used. And the interest rate on credit card debt is over 60%. You can see why the credit cards will soon cease working there. Inflation was expected to go over 100% in 2015 (which it did). Desperate consumers simply postpone paying their credit card debt, realizing that the inflation will run ahead of the interest rate.

Compounding at 100% a year will turn a $10,000 debt into $160,000 in five years. In 10 years, it will be over $5 million. **You don't have to be a mathematician to see that the credit card companies will pull the plug long before that happens.**

Credit stops when currency values become unpredictable or uncontrollable. And the resulting disaster is equal and opposite to the amount of credit that preceded it.

That's why the Argentine disaster was peanuts. The Zimbabwe catastrophe was trivial in comparison.

In both countries, the typical citizen had no mortgage payment to make. They had no credit card, either. They were used to using cash... and merchants were used to taking it.

And when their own cash went bad, they could switch to U.S. dollars... or British pounds... This time, it won't be that easy. Even if you could put your hands on euros, or yen, or renminbi... it probably wouldn't help you. Because the crisis is now global. (In fact, the spark will probably not come from the U.S... but from Japan. But we will come to that in a minute.)

Crucially... in Argentina and Zimbabwe... and Weimar Germany... there was plenty of cash around... People were used to saving cash... holding cash... and using it, even for large purchases, such as houses. When the credit system broke down... it made little difference to most people.

And look again at the financial crisis that took place in Germany in the early '20s. Then, credit cards hadn't even been invented... there was no consumer credit to speak of in any form... and most people still lived on farms. People in the cities were devastated. But life in the country continued much as it had before. Almost. Gangs of hunger-mad city folk roamed the nearby countryside, trying to find food. And woe to the farmer who stood in their way!

Now, in modern America, long, complex chains of production and distribution put food on your table.

More than nine out of 10 people live in cities or suburbs. Almost no one – not even the farmers themselves – can feed themselves from their own gardens on their own land. Instead, they all depend on credit.

The farmer uses credit to buy supplies, fuel, fertilizer... everything. The wholesaler, too, relies largely on credit to buy the raw food, process, and package it. The trucking industry uses credit to buy fuel. The retailer needs credit to keep the lights on and the stores open.

Six out of 10 customers pay for their groceries using credit cards. And don't forget America's huge underclass. About 47 million people depend on electronic transfers from the government to their SNAP (Supplemental Nutrition Assistance Program) cards. Typically, these people have very little cash on hand... and almost no provisions of food. What happens when the food stores stop taking their SNAP cards?

Over half a century, credit has replaced cash in America. There was only $1 trillion of total credit in America in 1965. And very few credit cards; they were only invented in 1958. Today, I take out my wallet and count seven plastic cards. And the total amount of outstanding credit is 50 times what it was in the mid-'60s. Our whole economy... and our way of life... have been shaped by this explosion of credit. We live on it. We depend on it.

So what happens when the credit stops? The whole production chain stops with it. Which is why the coming financial crisis in America could be much worse than any the world has ever known.

But let me be clear. The disaster we're looking at is not the collapse of the dollar... as so many analysts have forecast...

No, it's not that simple. The dollar will lose value. But as it loses value, people will be desperate to have it. Because they'll need dollars to pay their bills and to buy the things they need. They will be desperate to get rid of it, too... because a falling dollar is a threat to their wealth. Currencies have two main functions – transactions and savings. On both counts, the dollar will fail... but not immediately.

Economies breathe in and out. Inflation raises debt levels and prices. Deflation lowers them. Over the last 30 years, **the expansion of credit has pushed real dollars out of the economy.**

Today, the typical American has less than $20 in cash on hand. Women may carry giant handbags, but they have little cash in them – often less than $10.

I once boarded a plane for a round-the-world business trip with barely $25 in my wallet. I was confident that ATMs would work wherever I went. And they did.

But what if the ATMs no longer have the cash to give out?

CHAPTER 15
The Road We're Following

The major economies are so reliant on cheap credit that they can't give it up. We look to Japan, as the leader of the pack, to see what will happen next.

For 25 years, Japan has managed to maintain the status quo by inputting huge amounts of credit and printing-press money. Government debt went from 60% of GDP in 1989 to 245% in 2015. Government deficits have averaged about 3.4% of GDP, but are running at 6% in 2015.

While debt increased, GDP did not.

So the ratio of debt to the ability of the economy to pay has gotten worse and worse. While it earned $1.40 (GDP) for every dollar of public debt in 1989, at the time of this writing, the ratio is around 45 cents for every dollar of debt. And that is just the government debt. Altogether, the Japanese have debt equal to six times annual GDP – the highest in the world.

If the rate of interest on this debt were a "normal" 3% or so... it would pose a terrible dilemma. Nearly one out of every five dollars of output would be required just to pay the interest. The government, already running in the red, would see its deficits explode as 25% of its tax revenues would be required to service past debt.

Japan is going broke. First, because trade surpluses – Japan's traditional source of growth and funding – are now declining, from 612.7 billion yen to 11.4 billion yen (as of late 2014). Savings rates are falling, too – from 12% in 1995 to 1% in 2014. And to make matters finally and irretrievably catastrophic, the birthrate fell to 1.13 per woman by the end of 2014, which is so far below replacement level that whole towns are being emptied out – not to mention the labor pool. By 2030, there will be only two workers for every retired person.

Under these circumstances, growing the economy faster than the debt is not possible. Debt will continue to grow faster than income. And it will have to be financed by the Bank of Japan; that is, by cash and credit from nowhere.

Japan is ahead of us. But the road is the same. While the U.S. and Europe could still turn off – by cutting spending, substantially – that is unlikely to happen.

The typical household now gets more money from the government than it pays in taxes; it will be opposed to cuts. And elite policymakers still believe that cutting government spending leads to reduced demand and slower growth (making it even harder to "grow" out of debt).

That is why during the '07-'10 period, for example, U.S. GDP grew by only 4.26% while debt grew by 61%.

No Exit

America, Europe, and Japan all suffer from the same problems... and apply the same solutions. All are shackled to the ball and chain of debt, with their central banks adding to the weight.

To make matters worse, artificially low interest rates, bailouts, "back-stopping stock markets," and quantitative easing misdirect capital to inefficient and unproductive uses... further slowing real capital formation and prosperity.

These problems, in Europe and Japan, particularly, but in America, too, are exacerbated by falling rates of household formation and fertility. While the debts... and cost of social services... go up, there will be fewer people to pay them. None of the three major economies – given reasonable assumptions – can work its way down from the ledge. They cannot "grow their way out" of their debt problems. They will either jump... or be pushed.

We have never been in this situation before. Never have so many people depended on so much credit. Never has the world had so much debt. And never have so many central bankers done so much to pump up the global supply of "money."

The classical economists would be staggered to see it. If you could tell them about it, they probably wouldn't believe you. Still, they might help us understand where it leads.

Happily, we don't have to figure everything out ourselves. At least six generations of serious thinkers have studied, analyzed, and observed financial disasters. Ludwig von Mises, for example, was on the scene during Germany's hyperinflation of the 1920s. Here, he explains how the phenomenon develops:

> If once public opinion is convinced that the increase in the quantity of money will continue and never come to an end, and that consequently the prices of all commodities and services will not cease to rise, everybody becomes eager to buy as much as possible and to restrict his cash holding to a minimum size. For under these circumstances the regular costs incurred by holding cash are increased by the losses caused by the progressive fall in purchasing power.
>
> The advantages of holding cash must be paid for by sacrifices which are deemed unreasonably burdensome. This phenomenon was, in the great European inflations of the twenties, called flight into real goods (*Flucht in die Sachwerte*) or crack-up boom (*Katastrophenhausse*).

He could not comment on a breakdown in a credit-based system. No such system existed.

But note that the "flight into real goods" and the "crack-up boom" both anticipate the same thing: a big increase in the velocity of money. This is just what the central banks are hoping for.

They want you to spend your money rather than save it. And this is what they are likely to get, probably more than they were bargaining for.

Currently, prices are rising more slowly than the authorities would like.

Richard Duncan is chief economist at Blackhorse Asset Management in Singapore. He is also a friend of ours and an adviser to our family office. One of our editors, Chris Lowe, interviewed him recently.

Richard had an apt analogy:

> The global economy is like a big rubber raft. Instead of being inflated with air, it's inflated with credit plus commodities, including gold, and 7 billion people.
>
> The problem is the raft has now become fundamentally defective, flawed because so much credit has been created that the income of the 7 billion people is insufficient to service the interest on the debt, and they keep defaulting.
>
> When they default, the credit leaks outside of the raft.

People are not spending... not hiring... and not investing with much gusto. Just the opposite. There is no broad economic boom in any major economy. An increase in the velocity of money – which will lead to the kind of buying frenzy von Mises anticipated – is not even on the horizon.

Down... and Then Up

In 1978, Paul Volcker took over at the Fed. His plan was to jump. That is, he was willing to endure the pain of recession in order to bring inflation under control.

That was then. This is now. In 1978, the U.S. government owed $789 billion. Today, it owes $19.5 trillion. Then, interest rates were high. Now, they are low. Then, money was turning over too fast. Now, it stays put. Then, stocks were low. Now, they are high.

Then, Volcker and the U.S. political establishment could grit their teeth, raise rates, and get it over with. Now, the pain would be too much to bear.

Richard Duncan again:

> There's only one possible policy response and that's to pump in more credit. That's what the QE is about. They pump in more credit and when they do the raft reflates. Asset prices all go back up again and the people have dry feet and they're all happy again.

> What happens if they completely cut off the money printing now and don't step in with some other policy like more aggressive fiscal stimulus again, then the raft would sink just like it did in 1930. We would get sucked into a deflationary whirlpool and the international banking system would collapse and global trade would collapse.

Officials can't let the raft sink. Or they think they can't.

Paul Volcker was facilitating a natural turn in the credit market, from high yields to lower ones. Janet Yellen and her colleagues are desperately trying to prevent another major shift, from low yields to higher ones. No secret as to why. Were interest rates to go back to 7%, where U.S. mortgage rates were as recently as 2001, the interest on the government debt would take more than $1 trillion per year. It would be catastrophic!

The next phase of the drama is likely to come when stock prices fall heavily. U.S. stock prices have been going up for the last seven years. They are now so high that our in-house model, called DAMA – based on a retrospective of market cap to GDP, adjusted for debt and

---

demographics – predicts *negative* 7% per year from U.S. stocks over the next 10 years.

It hardly matters. We know stocks are always subject to occasional bear markets and crashes. We know that debt markets are subject to big losses, too – even as the Fed holds down interest rates. (Just ask a lender to the energy sector! JPMorgan Chase estimates that if oil prices stay low, 40% of all high-yield energy bonds could default.)

This is the future the Fed is firmly committed to preventing. To that end, I see four measures coming:

1. Direct and indirect equity purchases, designed to imitate a "wealth effect."

2. Direct money funding of government debts; central banks will buy government debt... perhaps all of it.

3. "Helicopter money" – bypassing the banking system, the feds will give tax credits to individual households, financed – along with huge new fiscal stimulus programs – by central banks.

4. Finally, the central banks will write off the government debt.

All of these initiatives have the same goal – to keep debt expanding rather than contracting. The first is ongoing in Japan... beginning in Europe... and "on hold" in the U.S. The second is underway in Japan... still not engaged in other major economies. The third will only come out after a major negative shock to the system. The fourth will happen when the other options are exhausted.

The last of these was suggested by economist Richard Koo of Nomura Securities in Tokyo. It is his solution to the Japanese debt problem. Since so much of the debt is owned by the central bank... and since the central bank is an arm of the government... the debt can be written off, no harm, no foul.

At first glance, this seems to be a real solution. All of a sudden, the debt disappears. And nobody is worse off. Now, the government can borrow more money from the central bank... on and on... forever and ever. Amen.

It sounds too good to be true. And it is. What has actually happened? The government has absorbed real assets and paid for them without collecting taxes. It has simply printed pieces of paper (or the electronic equivalent). And nobody is worse off?

If this really could be done, every country in the world would run its public finances this way. But von Mises tells us why central bankers who don't jump eventually get pushed off the ledge:

> ...then, finally, the masses wake up. They become suddenly aware of the fact that inflation is a deliberate policy and will go on endlessly. A breakdown occurs. The crack-up boom appears. Everybody is anxious to swap his money against "real" goods, no matter whether he needs them or not, no matter how much money he has to pay for them.
>
> Within a very short time, within a few weeks or even days, the things which were used as money are no longer used as media of exchange. They become scrap paper. Nobody wants to give away anything against them.

Today's money won't even help you start a campfire. It is credit, not paper. In our imagined future, this credit will go bad when the breakdown occurs.

This is the future central banks are working so hard to prevent. It is where the can is kicked... the future no one wants. No one plans for it. No one is ready for it.

And yet, it is the future we should all be prepared for.

To Answer Your Question...

No one can know what will happen. But you should be prepared to meet the future the feds claim they can avoid.

Remember, a crack-up boom can send good assets up to hallucinogenic levels. Good companies survive, and can even prosper. Good real estate remains. Bonds – good and bad – do not.

The simplest and easiest thing to do today is to make sure you have a supply of real money – cash.

Have on hand some silver bullion coins for transactional purposes. Keep some for savings, too.

Stay diversified, with 10% to 40% of your wealth in real money (gold)... and the rest in real estate and solid stocks.

Keep a healthy supply of food and necessities on hand, too. If the supply chain breaks down – unlikely perhaps, but possible – many people will be desperate. You don't want to be among them.

I know it is not practical for everyone, but it is also a good idea to have a small farm or rural property where you can wait out a real crisis. Food, water, a fireplace and a woodpile... a few gold coins... friends and family...

Hey, what more do you need?

CHAPTER 16

Why Are We in This Mess?

We have bad news and good news.

The good news is that there will be no 25-year recession. Nor will there be a depression that will last the rest of our lifetimes. The bad news: It will be much worse than that.

"A long depression" has been much discussed in the financial press. Several economists are predicting many years of sluggish or negative growth. It is the obvious consequence of several overlapping trends and existing conditions.

First, people are getting older. Especially in Europe and Japan, but also in China, Russia, and the U.S.

As we've described many times, as people get older, they change. They stop producing and begin consuming. They are no longer the dynamic innovators and eager early adopters of their youth; they become the old dogs who won't learn new tricks.

Nor are they the green and growing timber of a healthy economy; instead, they become deadwood.

There's nothing wrong with growing old. There's nothing wrong with dying, either, at least from a philosophical point of view. But it's not going to increase auto sales or boost incomes – except for the undertakers.

Second, most large economies are deeply in debt. The increase in debt levels began after World War II and sped up after the money system changed in 1968-71.

By 2007, U.S. consumers reached what was probably "peak debt." That is, they couldn't continue to borrow and spend as they had for the previous half-century. Most of their debt was mortgage debt, and the price of housing was falling.

The feds reacted as they always do... inappropriately. They tried to cure a debt problem with more debt. But consumers were both unwilling and unable to borrow. Their incomes and their collateral were going down. This left corporations and government to aim only for their own toes.

Central banks created more money and credit – trillions of dollars of it. But since the household sector wasn't borrowing, the money went into financial assets and zombie government spending. Neither provided any significant support for wages or output. So, the real economy went soft, even as the cost of credit fell to its lowest levels in history.

Third, the developed economies have been zombified. The U.S., for example, is way down at No. 46 on the World Bank's list of places where it is easiest to start a new business (at the time of writing). And only one G8 country – Canada – even makes the top 10.

Paperwork. Expenses. Regulation. High taxes. High labor rates. Entrenched competition with aging, loyal customers. All are endemic; from Boston to Berlin to Beijing.

Leading industries – heavily controlled and regulated, including defense, education, health, and finance – are practically arms of the government. All are protected with high barriers to entry and low expectations. Competition is barely tolerated. Innovation is discouraged. Mistakes are forgiven and reimbursed.

Meanwhile, the masses are encouraged to become zombies, too, with generous rewards for those who 1) do nothing, 2) pretend to work, or 3) prevent other people from doing anything. After all the zombies, cronies, and connivers get their money, there is little left for the productive economy.

The Solution Begins When Markets Crack

Typically, these problems – too much debt, too many zombies, and too many old people – lead to financial crises. Then, they are "solved" by either inflation or depression. And the solution begins when markets crack.

Markets never go up forever. Instead, they go up, down, and even sideways. They breathe in and out. And after sucking in air for the last 30 years, U.S. financial assets are ready to exhale. Legendary asset manager Bill Gross comments:

> When does our credit-based financial system sputter/break down?
>
> When investable assets pose too much risk for too little return.
>
> Not immediately, but at the margin, credit and stocks begin to be exchanged for figurative and sometimes literal money in a mattress.

When that happens, problems begin to take care of themselves, in one of two ways...

A quick, sharp depression wipes out the value of credit claims. Borrowers go broke. Bonds expire worthless. Companies declare bankruptcy. The whole capital structure tends to get marked down as debts are written off and financial assets of all kinds lose their value.

Or, under pressure, the feds print money. Debts are diminished as the currency loses its value. The zombies still get money, but it is worth less. Inflation adjustments cannot keep up with high rates of inflation. Pensions, prices, and promises fade.

Either way, the slate is wiped clean and a new cycle can begin.

But what rag will clean the slate now?

In early May 2015, our proprietary short-term stock market indicator has turned starkly negative, as shown below:

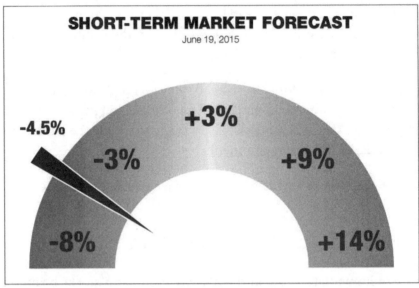

www.bonnerandpartners.com

The near-term outlook is clearly darkening. Based on simple regression-to-the-mean logic, our model now suggests that the "most likely" course for U.S. stocks through the end of the summer is a loss of more than 6%.

As to the long-term outlook...

The bad news is much worse. The logic of the "long depression" is simple: aging populations, debt, zombification – all of which slow growth. How many old people and zombies do you need before an economy comes to a halt?

Nobody knows. But the drag from debt is observable and calculable.

Over the last three decades, approximately $33 trillion in excess debt has been contracted – above and beyond the traditional ratio to income – in America alone. And growth rates have fallen in half.

That's because dollars that would otherwise support current

spending are instead used to pay for past spending. Our old debts have to be retired with current income.

The money doesn't disappear, of course. Some goes to creditors who spend it. Some comes back as capital investment, which is a form of spending. But as credit shrinks, generally, so does the economy.

And that brings us to the impossible situation we're in now. In order to get back to a healthy ratio – say approximately $1.50 worth of debt for every $1 in income – you'd need to erase all that excess that has already been contracted.

In other words, you'd have to take $1 trillion out of the consumer economy every year for the next 33 years. It would be the longest and deepest depression in U.S. history.

A Credit Crisis, Complete with Howling, Whining, and Finger-Pointing

Take a trillion out of the U.S. economy and you have a 4% decline in GDP. Then, as the economy declines, the remaining debt burden becomes even heavier.

Try to pay down debt and it becomes harder and harder to pay down.

You stop buying in order to save money. Your local merchants lose sales. Then they try to cut expenses, and you lose your job.

In other words, no "steady state slump" is possible. When the credit cycle turns, it will not be a gentle slope, but a catastrophic cliff... a credit crisis, complete with howling, whining, finger-pointing... and more clumsy rescue efforts from the feds.

There are two solutions to a debt crisis: Inflation or deflation.

Central banks can cause asset price inflation. But it is not always as easy as it looks. Consumer price inflation requires the willing cooperation of households.

With little borrowing and spending from the household sector, credit remains in the banks and the financial sector. Asset prices soar. Consumer prices barely move.

U.S. consumer price inflation over the course of 2014, for example, was approximately zero.

The assumption behind the "long depression" hypothesis is that central banks cannot or will not be able to cause an acceptable or desirable level of consumer price inflation. As a result, the economy will be stuck with low inflation, low (sometimes negative) growth, and low bond yields.

But what about deflation? If inflation won't reduce debt, why not let deflation do the job?

CHAPTER 17

Deflation Works!

We've been exploring how the credit bubble resolves itself. Inflation? Deflation? Are we locked into a long, long period of stagnation, slump, and economic sclerosis?

First, we give you our long-term forecast:

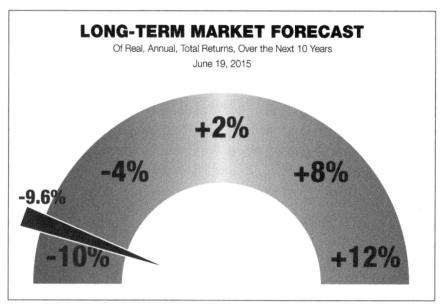

LONG-TERM MARKET FORECAST
Of Real, Annual, Total Returns, Over the Next 10 Years
June 19, 2015

+2%
-4%   +8%
-9.6%
-10%   +12%

"This is the most negative ever," says our chief number cruncher Stephen Jones. It shows a loss of 9.8% every year for the next 10 years. In other words, our mean-regressing, debt/demography-adapted model seems to be pointing to a long depression.

But an average loss of 9.8% per year over 10 years can happen in a number of different ways. Little by little. Or in one savage blow.

A foreshadow of the long depression crossed the planet like a total eclipse of the sun twice in the last 100 years.

The first time was America's Great Depression. You know that story. Stocks crashed. Businesses went broke. People lost their jobs. Banks failed. Events were following the typical depression script, which probably would have bottomed out and recovered within a couple of years – as happened in the depression of 1921.

But then, the federal government stepped in. It froze prices, including the price of labor. It cut off trade. It blocked liquidations. It arrested the progress of the correction.

Murray Rothbard analyzed the policies of the Hoover and Roosevelt administrations in his 1963 classic, *America's Great Depression*. He showed how government, trying to stop the Depression, actually prevented it from doing its work.

The short, quick deflationary shock – which should have slashed bad debt, bad businesses, and bad investments – turned into a long, agonizing slump. The Depression, which should have been over by 1933, continued until the 1940s and was only ended then by the biggest public works spending program in history – World War II.

This, by the way, did not actually make people better off economically, but it "put people to work" and largely disguised the drop in living standards which that war and the Depression had caused.

The second long depression was in Japan, following the crash of its stock market in 1990. It has now been a quarter of a century since that crash. Japanese GDP has scarcely advanced, as you can see in the next chart.

And the Japanese stock market?

From a high of nearly 40,000 in 1990, at the time of writing, the Nikkei index now trades at around 20,000. It's taken 25 years to claw itself back to a 50% loss!

The blame for the length of the depression can be placed squarely on the government. To this day, it continues to meddle in the economy – essentially forestalling a genuine cleanup of bad debt.

Instead of allowing the bad debt to be written off and reduced, policymakers have added more and more debt over the entire 25-year period so that today, Japan's government is the most indebted in the world.

And now Japan is running out of time and money. Its aging population is no longer saving for retirement; now retirees expect to spend those savings. This means that the government can no longer count on financing from Japan's savers. Now it must return their money.

Real GDP Growth: 1991-2012 (1991=100)

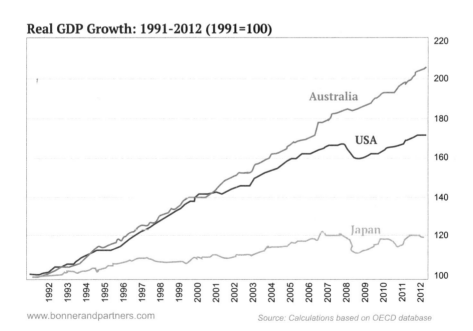

www.bonnerandpartners.com   *Source: Calculations based on OECD database*

But how? It has no money to give them. Like the U.S., it has been running budget deficits for years.

Japan's economy is in a crisis. It's been two years since the Shinzō Abe government began its stimulus program. But wages are actually lower today than they were when it began. And this is happening against a backdrop of falling labor supply: The labor pool is expected to shrink by 20% over the next 25 years. The main goal of the stimulus program was to raise Japan's inflation rate. But you could multiply price increases of 2014 by nine and still not reach the government's 2% target.

In the U.S., too, inflation has been disappearing as fast as good manners. In 2014, consumer prices were approximately flat. And that is despite a 400% increase in the Fed's assets – the nation's money foundation – over the last six years.

If that kind of money printing doesn't cause an increase in the CPI, what would? We'll come back to that question in a minute.

Cheap Credit Keeps the Wheels Turning

If inflation can't be counted on to reduce the world's debts, what about deflation?

The feds fear it, loathe it, and try to prevent it every way they can. But deflation works. It knocks down sales, prices, and employment, forcing borrowers into bankruptcy. Then, their debts are worthless.

Alas, in a zero-rate world, the banana peels disappear from the sidewalks. It is almost impossible to go broke, default, or fall on your face.

Grant's Interest Rate Observer told the story of one company: RadioShack. The company lost the plot back in 2007, says *Grant's*. *The Onion* satirized its chief executive, Julian Day, putting the following words in his mouth:

There must be some sort of business model that enables this company to make money, but I'll be damned if I know what it is.

But RadioShack stayed in business – borrowing even more money as its credit rating declined from BB to D (or "junk") over the following eight years. Finally, it bit the dust in February of this year.

There's nothing like unlimited cheap credit to keep the wheels turning – slowly. In 2009, a grim year for American business, 60,837 firms declared bankruptcy. In 2014, there were 26,983 bankruptcies.

What is surprising is not that there were so few, but that there were so many. When you can borrow for nothing... or close to nothing... why does anyone ever default?

Of course, not all firms have equal access to the free money. The little guys go broke. The big guys stay in business. The economy stays alive, but on life support.

The big limitation of this system is that as the slump worsens, prices fall and real interest rates actually go up. That is, the feds may lend at zero, but if prices are falling, the effective, real borrowing rate may rise.

The authorities would be "zero-bound," unable to take nominal rates below zero and unable to keep the real price of money at nothing.

Until recently, it had been presumed that rates could not sink below zero. People would not pay for the privilege of holding cash in a bank or a bond; they would just take the cash and hoard it.

But all over the world, central governments have begun a "War on Cash" designed to force people to use credit rather than cash. The feds can monitor, tax, and control credit. They can even force you to pay for the privilege of having it.

The European Central Bank and the Swiss National Bank already require depositors to pay for storing money. And beginning this week, JPMorgan Chase began charging depositors a "utilization fee" to hold their money.

Meanwhile, economists are advocating taxing cash or even, like Harvard economics professor Ken Rogoff, making it illegal. France has already made it illegal to make payments of more than €1,000 with cash. Sweden is currently removing cash from all ATMs. And the U.S. requires financial industry workers – such as bank tellers – to rat out customers by filing "suspicious activity reports" on anyone who comes in with what they consider an inappropriately large amount of cash.

Why the "War on Cash"?

Partly to control you. And partly to control the economy. If they can create a NIRP world – with negative nominal interest rates – they may be able to keep the credit flowing to cronies and zombies, maintaining the economy in a coma for many years.

Businesses that should go broke will have access to credit. Speculators will still make money. Governments will continue to print money and borrow it from themselves. The zombies will throw rocks and bottles every once in a while, but they will still get their cash and the system will survive.

Long, drawn-out depressions are caused by governments.

The politicians respond to today's capital interests, not tomorrow's. Today's retirees vote. Today's stockholders give campaign contributions. Today's cronies control the power and money of today's society.

And all of them fear one thing more than any other: the future.

They all know they will die, and that the process of capitalism is creative destruction – today's wealth owners must be stripped of their money and power so that tomorrow's generations can take over. And that's why the government's essential role is to look into the future and prevent it from happening.

This is just another way of saying that governments will always try to stop depressions, because depressions are creative destruction in action.

Capitalism chops down today's trees so that tomorrow's saplings can get some air and light.

But trying to stop creative destruction does not stop the future. It just changes it.

Instead of a dynamic, honest, and growing economy, we get stagnation, economic gangrene, and financial rigor mortis. Long depressions, in other words.

CHAPTER 18

Don't Expect the Fed to Sit Tight

As we have seen, Japan has already had a 25-year slump. The U.S. is now in Year 8 of its slump, with fragile growth at only half the rate of the last century. They could get better... or worse.

Negative rates could keep the cronies in business. The slump itself – combined with peak debt and 500 million Chinese laborers – could keep inflation in check.

But the point comes when investors see that the risk of loss (because something can always go wrong) is greater than the hope of gain. That moment must be approaching in the U.S. stock market. Prices are near record highs, even as the economy flirts with recession.

One day, perhaps soon, we will see stocks falling – as much as 1,000 points in 24 hours.

Jacking up the stock market has been the Fed's singular success. Activism has been its creed. Interventionism is its modus operandi. It will not sit tight as the market falls apart and the economy goes into recession. Instead, it will announce QE4. It will try to enforce negative interest rates. And it will move – as will the Japanese – to "direct monetary funding" of government deficits.

That is, it will dispense with the fiction of "borrowing" from its own central bank. It will simply print the money it needs.

The U.S. Fed of 1930 was not nearly as ambitious and assertive as the Fed of 2015. In the '30s, it watched as the economy chilled into a Great Depression. As Ben Bernanke told Milton Friedman, "We won't do that again."

It couldn't if it wanted to. Back in the '30s, consumer debt had barely been invented. Most people still lived on or near farms, where they could take care of themselves even if the economy was in a depression. Few people had credit. Instead, they had savings. There were no food stamps. No disability. No rent assistance. No zombie industries. No student debt. No auto debt. No cashback mortgages. And cash was real money backed by gold.

Today, a long depression in the U.S. would be unbearable. The public couldn't stand it. Six out of 10 households live paycheck to paycheck. Can you imagine what would happen if those paychecks ceased?

Supposedly, the U.S. economy is still growing... with the stock market near record highs. Yet, one out of every five households in America has not a single wage earner. Among inner-city black men ages 20-24, only four out of 10 have jobs. Half the households in the U.S. count on government money to make ends meet. And 50 million get food stamps.

What would happen to the cities – and the suburbs – in a real depression? What would Janet Yellen do? Would she repeat the words of Andrew Mellon in 1929 to "liquidate labor, liquidate stocks, liquidate the farmers, liquidate real estate..."?

According to Mellon, this would "purge the rottenness out of the system. High costs of living and high living will come down. People will work harder, live a more moral life. Values will be adjusted, and enterprising people will pick up from less competent people."

Mellon was just suggesting that creative destruction be allowed to do its job. He was the last Treasury secretary to make such a forthright and honest comment. Thenceforth, Treasury secretaries and central bank governors could no longer accept the tough love of a free-enterprise economy. They had to offer bogus rehab and claptrap therapy. They had to stop creative destruction. They had to "tell it like it wasn't" because that's the way people wanted it. They had to pretend to make a better world by improving the market economy.

We Need Another Mellon

Today, a central banker or Treasury secretary who let deflation purge the rottenness from the system would be dismissed before sundown. Too much wealth, too many reputations, too much power and status depends on the continuation of the credit expansion. Instead of a Mellon, we will have a Greenspan, a Bernanke, or a Yellen. And we will soon find out whether Mr. Bernanke spoke the truth in 2002 when he said:

> *We conclude that, under a paper-money system, a determined government can always generate higher spending and hence positive inflation.*

Threatened with deflation, the authorities will want to turn the tide in the worst possible way. What's the worst way to stop deflation? With hyperinflation.

Yes, we may suffer a year or two more of sluggish growth... or even deflation. Stocks will crash and people will be desperate for paper dollars. But sooner or later, the feds will find their feet and lose their heads.

Most likely, the credit-drenched world will end... not with a whimper of deflation, but with a bang. Hyperinflation will bring the long depression to a dramatic close long before a quarter of a century has passed.

PART 4

On Surviving (and Prospering)
in the Age of Dying Credit

CHAPTER 19

Crisis Money Guide

In the last crisis, every major bank and investment firm on Wall Street would have gone broke had the feds not intervened. Next time, it might not be so easy to save them.

The next crisis is likely to be across ALL asset classes. And with $57 trillion more in global debt than in 2007, it is likely to be much harder to stop.

Are you with us so far?

Because here is where it gets interesting...

In a gold-backed monetary system, prices fall. But the money is still there. Money becomes more valuable. It doesn't disappear. It is more valuable because you can use it to buy more stuff.

Naturally, people hold on to it. Of course, the velocity of money – the frequency at which each unit of currency is used to buy something – falls. And this makes it appear that the supply of money is falling, too.

But imagine what happens to credit money. The money doesn't just stop circulating. It vanishes.

A bank that had an "asset" (in the form of a loan to a customer) of $100,000 in June might have zilch by July. A corporation that splurged on share buybacks one week could find those shares cut in half two weeks later. A person with a $100,000 stock market portfolio one day could find his portfolio has no value at all a few days later.

All of this is standard fare for a credit crisis. The new wrinkle – a

---

devastating one – is that people now do what they always did, but they are forced to do it in a radically different way.

They stop spending. They hoard cash. But what cash do you hoard when most transactions are done on credit? Do you hoard a line of credit? Do you put your credit card in your vault?

No. People will hoard the kind of cash they understand... something they can put their hands on... something that is gaining value – rapidly. They'll want dollar bills.

Also, following a well-known pattern, these paper dollars will quickly disappear. People drain cash machines. They drain credit facilities. They ask for "cash back" when they use their credit cards. They want real money – old-fashioned money that they can put in their pockets and their home safes...

Dollar Panic

Let us stop here and remind readers that we're talking about a short time frame – days... maybe weeks... a couple of months at most. That's all. It's the period after the credit crisis has sucked the cash out of the system... and before the government's inflation tsunami has hit.

As Ben Bernanke put it, "a determined central bank can always create positive consumer price inflation." But it takes time!

And during that interval, panic will set in. A dollar panic – with people desperate to put their hands on dollars to pay for food... for fuel... and for everything else they need.

Credit might still be available. But it will be useless. No one will want it. ATMs and banks will run out of cash. Credit facilities will be drained of real cash. Banks will put up signs. First: "Cash withdrawals limited to $500." And then: "No cash withdrawals."

You will have a credit card with a $10,000 line of credit. You have $5,000 in your debit account. But all financial institutions are staggering. And in the news, you will read that your bank has defaulted and been placed in receivership. What would you rather have? Your $10,000 line of credit or a stack of $50 bills?

You will go to buy gasoline. You will take out your credit card to pay.

"Cash only," the sign will say. Because the machinery of the credit economy will be breaking down. The gas station... its suppliers... and its financiers do not want to get stuck with "credit" from your bankrupt lender!

Whose lines of credit are still valuable? Whose bank is ready to fail? Who can pay his mortgage? Who will honor his credit card debt? In a crisis, those questions will be as common as "Who will win an Oscar?" is today.

But no one will know the answers. Quickly, they will stop guessing... and turn to cash.

Our advice: Keep some cash on hand. You might need it.

But what if you don't have any physical cash on hand? What if the ATMs are shut down? What if your credit cards stop working? And what if you can't even cash a check?

This nightmare scenario is not only possible... it's happened many times before. Just look at the recent examples of Argentina and Greece, and you'll see how easily cash can vanish.

When that happens, it's crucial to know about cash alternatives.

CHAPTER 20

Cash Alternative: Gold Jewelry

With limited options, one early dollar substitute could turn out to be gold and silver in the form of jewelry or small-denomination gold coins. A good course of action here is to collect and assess any small gold chains and charms you already own. This is exactly what happened, for instance, in Argentina during that country's most recent financial collapse.

Remember, a gold chain purchased at Walmart and labeled 18-karat gold will be just as valuable as the same chain bought at a fancy department store or jewelry shop. You just won't have paid a stiff markup for workmanship that will be meaningless later. The gold weight matters most.

However, do not rush to buy gold jewelry at retail outlets. Even at discount chains, the markup on jewelry can be significant compared to straight gold in the form of coins.

For instance, a men's necklace currently sold at Walmart for $397 weighs 4.28 grams. It's 14-karat gold. That means it's just a bit over half gold, or 2.5 grams' worth. At current prices, a gram of gold is worth $38, so that $397 necklace has just $95 worth of gold inside it!

Another way of looking at it: Gold would have to quadruple in price to overcome the markup on that necklace. You start out in a deep hole. Better to buy used jewelry and know its true gold value first.

You might find better deals in pawnshops – if you know how to negotiate. Pawnbrokers deal in gold jewelry often, but they have significantly fewer up-front costs in acquiring the pieces they then attempt to sell. You are in a better position by far.

If you do buy jewelry, try to buy gold marked at least 18 karats by weight. That means the piece is 75% gold. If you have 24-karat pieces, those are 100% gold, not an alloy. Either form will work, but it's important that they are marked clearly and that you know the exact weight of each piece of jewelry.

You can always check a small piece by turning it over and finding the karat weight stamp, then weighing the item on a small pocket scale before buying.

Be forewarned, measures are tricky when it comes to gold. An electronic jeweler's scale is a good investment. Jewelers use a measurement standard known as a troy ounce. A normal electronic scale is likely to read an ounce as a little more than 28.3 grams, while a troy ounce is 31.1 grams.

You also might see gold measured in pennyweight (dwt) as a division of a troy ounce. There are 20 pennyweights in a troy ounce, while 1 pennyweight is 1.555 grams. Here's a conversion table to help make things clear:

	U.S. ounce	Troy ounce	Pennyweight	Gram
U.S. ounce	1	1.097	0.055	0.0353
Troy ounce	0.911	1	0.05	0.0321
Pennyweight	18.229	20	1	0.643
Gram	28.350	31.103	1.555	1

Look for a small stamp on the back of your gold jewelry pieces. You might need a jeweler's spyglass, or loupe, or a standard magnifying glass to see it. The karat weight will be expressed in decimals or as a number followed by the letter K.

Consider that 24-karat means 100% gold, and that all lesser weights mean some part of the piece is non-gold metal meant to strengthen the item and make it durable. The calculation always adds up to 24 parts, while the designation only tells you what fraction is real gold.

If it's 18-karat gold, then you might see this written as 0.750, meaning 75% gold. If you check your math, 18 is 75% of 24.

Weight	Stamp	Decimals	Amount of Gold
10 karats	10K	0.417	10 parts gold + 14 parts other metals
14 karats	14K	0.585	14 parts gold + 10 parts other metals
18 karats	18K	0.750	18 parts gold + 6 parts other metals
24 karats	24K	1.0	24 parts gold + zero parts other metals

CHAPTER 21

How to Own Gold

If you plan to build up a supply of gold for barter, it's very important to understand the process of gold buying well before you need to buy it. Gold coins, for instance, have a dealer markup just like jewelry, only much smaller. Dealers have to make a living, after all.

You can negotiate discounts for larger purchases, but remember that a gold bar that weighs 400 troy ounces (27.5 pounds) will not be a help later unless you can somehow divide it. Your buyer might not want a hacked-off hunk of gold as much as a clearly valued gold coin he can resell easily.

Real, pure gold is 99.5% gold in its bullion form. There are a variety of ways to test the purity of gold, ranging from fast and easy to harder but more certain.

For instance, you can check a gold ring or necklace easily with a magnet. Gold is not magnetic. If the piece moves toward a magnet, then it might be just gold in color or lightly plated with gold.

Likewise, you can test gold by rubbing it on an unglazed ceramic plate, such as a terra cotta planter dish. Real gold will rub off on the ceramic, while base metals will leave a black mark. Note, however, that rubbing the piece will scratch it, and you still won't know how much of the piece is gold (its karat weight), only that it contains some gold.

Another easy (damage-free) test is to weigh the gold. Real gold of 24-karat purity will be 19 grams to the milliliter of water displaced. To check this, use a beaker with precise milliliter marks. For instance, if you put the gold in the beaker and it displaces 3 milliliters of water while weighing 57 grams, then 57 divided by three is 19.

Now you know that the object you have is at least the same density as pure gold. It might still not be gold, but now you know for a fact that it is heavy enough to be the real thing. If you know the density is right, you can be completely assured by conducting a simple acid test. A drop of nitric acid on real gold will not react, while lesser metals will result in various chemical reactions.

If you see colors such as green (an indicator of base metal presence), gold (gold-plated brass), or a milky color (gold-plated silver), then it's not pure gold.

What if the Government Confiscates Gold?

Sounds crazy, but it's part of our history. On January 30, 1934, Franklin D. Roosevelt signed the Gold Reserve Act, forcing U.S. citizens to relinquish their bullion to the government.

Coins were illegal, bullion bars forbidden. Rather than redeeming dollars for gold (the normal practice of the time), the banking system was turned inside out. Banks and citizens had to redeem their now-illegal gold for paper U.S. dollars. It could happen again, for any reason the government might choose, and at any time.

If that happens, you have to know how to assess, accumulate, and spend alternative currencies, as we explain in the rest of this guide.

But first, let's talk about what makes a good currency. Aristotle, the Greek philosopher, said the ideal form of money must contain four key attributes: durability, portability, divisibility, and intrinsic value. In his eyes, gold is the ideal form of money as it fits all four criteria:

- **Durability:** Aristotle was referring to money's ability to endure time, specifically its resistance to corrosion or fading. Gold was, naturally, the best choice at the time – and it still is. Some tribes used clay coins or shells as currency. But these became brittle and eroded over time, making them a bad store of wealth. Today, paper money is popular, but bills erode if not handled properly. In fact, the average U.S. bill spends only six years in circulation.

- **Portability:** A medium of exchange will not work if you can't easily pass it to someone. Can you imagine trying to pay for a car with bushels of corn? You'd need about 3,000 bushels – or 210,000 pounds – of corn for a $15,000 car. Or you could pay with less than a pound of gold.

- **Divisibility:** For anything to function as a currency, it must be easily divisible. What if you had a 100-ounce bar of gold and wanted to buy that $15,000 car? You could cut off the proper amount, weigh it to verify, and the transaction would be complete. If that seems like too much work, you can buy coins with 1 ounce of gold in them for this transaction.

- **Intrinsic Value:** The ideal currency should have value in and of itself or be hard to make. This makes precious metals good currencies. They have many industrial and decorative uses. Precious metals also have intrinsic value because you can't make more of them – you have to mine them. Imagine what would happen to the value of gold if you could whip it up in your kitchen just as easily as baking a batch of cookies. This is where the U.S. dollar loses credibility as a currency. The dollar is backed by nothing other than the "full faith and credit of the U.S. government." If that faith disappears, so does the value of the dollar.

CHAPTER 22

Alternative Mediums of Exchange

Beyond gold coins, jewelry, and bullion, what else will be of value?

Here are some non-metal stores of value to consider. These are not money, per se, but resources that will be of value if societal order is stressed to the breaking point:

Gold Receipts: An early progenitor of paper money was, in fact, a receipt for stored gold held by a depositor. In the 17th century, that was goldsmiths. (The modern equivalent is a mutual fund that issues shares based on stored gold.)

It's possible that such a system might be revived, creating an alternative "paper" currency backed by actual gold held in safekeeping. If so, gold receipts could be exchanged for goods and services, providing a form of hard money that otherwise would not exist.

This is not to suggest that you should attempt to purchase mutual-fund shares backed by gold. First of all, getting the actual paper certificates in the age of electronic storage will be impractical, and they could easily be faked. It will also be hard to estimate the real value of gold day-to-day if the economy collapses.

However, if enough people have large amounts of bullion that they cannot otherwise divide or trade, and they need some divisible medium of exchange for it, such a system might spring up locally (assuming clarity on the value of gold is available).

U.S. Postage: The scramble for paper of value might lead to dollar substitutes you might not expect. For instance, a "Forever" postage stamp has a quantifiable value today that is automatically and permanently adjusted for inflation, at least under current law.

The rate for a first-class letter today is 49 cents, so you can easily deduce that two stamps are worth about $1, four stamps are worth about $2, and so on. There is no reason to divide them, since they come in strips of 10 and 20 and even rolls of 10,000 (currently worth $4,900).

You wouldn't buy these to use them for postage. Rather, they are an assignment of value that is easy to agree on and protected from devaluation, in theory, forever.

Naturally, the U.S. Postal Service could ask Congress to cut off the supply of "Forever" stamps or change the regulation, but, in an intermediate period of no-value money, it would be easy for stamp holders to use them as reliable local scrip. The government might let this happen in order to avoid a total social breakdown.

Local Scrip: Locally issued paper money is a time-honored form of "emergency" currency designed to keep a small economy functional in tough times. During the 1990 recession, for instance, you could earn "Ithaca HOURS" in Ithaca, New York, by performing labor or supplying a handmade good, say, a knitted sweater.

Today in Bavaria, Germany, residents use chiemgauer notes, which they buy with euros but cannot spend outside the local towns. These notes lose value automatically if not spent, thanks to a 2% monthly fee charged by local banks. This is done in order to discourage speculation and hoarding. That feature, known as "demurrage," shows up in local currency schemes on and off throughout history.

The idea of local currencies pops up around the world for different reasons – from ritzy artist colonies in the Berkshires to poor urban areas of London, such as Brixton – but they all have the same goal: to keep a small economy working completely outside the boundaries of a larger one. This trend dates back to the Great Depression, when gigantic barter systems were common and scrip was created in order to facilitate exchanges when there was no one-to-one match. For instance, a farmer with a basket of apples might have needed to have a tool sharpened, while the tool sharpener really needed a pound of bacon, not apples.

Much like paper currency, the locally sanctioned scrip preserves the value of the basket of apples by substituting for it in the short term. It really couldn't earn interest or compound. It just smooths the way for more systematic bartering. Scrip bartering resurfaced in a big way in Argentina during the most recent economic collapse there, keeping the local economy afloat for millions of otherwise destitute Argentines.

Barter Currency: Bartering is difficult. Figuring out what you can do for your neighbor and what he can do for you is tough... and time-consuming. If your neighbor builds you a table, how many times would you have to mow his lawn for it to be a fair trade?

Or a more drastic example: Your family just ran out of food and you have no cash. But you have a gold watch on your wrist. The local food dealer senses desperation and asks for that watch in exchange for a week's worth of sandwiches. Would you make this trade or let your kids go hungry? In normal times, that watch would be worth the equivalent of two years' worth of food, but not now...

Barter currencies appeared centuries ago to help get around these dilemmas. A barter currency is essentially an IOU passed from person to person. These alternative currencies allow you to accept payment for your goods or services. Then you can purchase what you need elsewhere.

The most popular barter currency today is the Greek TEM. The TEM started in 2010 in the city of Volos in response to a looming currency shortage. Unemployment was over 20%. If the government cut spending, more jobs would be lost.

The only way some people could afford to buy anything was to barter their skills. So TEM's founders created this currency for local use.

To use TEMs, an individual or business must go to a TEM official and sign up for "the network." Each person gets an account with an online login. Similar to an online bank account, users can see their balance and transfer TEMs to others.

Electronic transfers aren't the only way to exchange TEMs. Individuals and merchants carry little slips of paper to record transactions. The buyer and seller just write down their information and the amount of the transaction. Later, someone enters the transaction into the network.

Eventually, all TEM transactions are recorded in an electronic ledger. This online database is part of the public record. While it might seem like an invasion of privacy, since everyone can view your TEM balance, it's not. Your entire wealth is probably not publicized, as each person is limited to 1,200 TEMs.

And there are benefits to having this information public – you can see if the people you are dealing with have enough TEMs to pay you. This will help ensure you don't get ripped off.

TEM's founders made it easy for businesses to accept either euros or TEMs; each TEM is worth one euro. If you order a coffee from the local café, you can pay €3, 3 TEMs, or a combination of the two.

Look out for these currencies springing up during a crisis.

Rations: Military surplus Meals, Ready-to-Eat (MREs) are surprisingly high-quality. And you can store a lot of them if you have a basement or other cool, dry place. Consider building up a supply that will last for several weeks. It might be easier to add MREs to your weekly shopping list and make a stop at the local army-navy surplus store to stock up while there is little demand.

It's very hard to quantify the value of readily consumable food to people who are not hungry now. If you do decide to stockpile rations for the future, you have to make sure you have the space to store them safely and securely. Don't advertise that you are sitting on months' worth of food.

If you choose to store just enough to tide your family over in the event of a temporary disruption in the economy or a natural disaster, your basement or other cool, dry underground space should be sufficient. The Red Cross recommends three days' worth of food (nonperishable) per person and a can opener, as well as 1 gallon of clean bottled water per person per day.

If you expect to do something on a larger scale, consider a climate-controlled storage space or your own small business storage, if you have that. Another strategy, if you have land, is to build an underground, weather-tight storage space just for rations. A ready-made underground tornado shelter, for instance, can function as a food-storage area if you make it large enough to accommodate your family and your food supply as needed.

Ammunition: If you don't have black powder, bullet casings, tools, and know-how, you can bet you will be paying someone else for fresh ammo. This is not to suggest a total breakdown is likely. It's possible, of course, but the bigger concern is being able to steadily hunt for protein from wild sources.

While hobbyists and arms enthusiasts will focus on the more exotic, highly powered firearms, the higher demand will be for common small-caliber bullets used in hunting, such as .22-caliber bullets. This was exactly the caliber bullet that was in short supply for several years starting in 2008.

Part of the reason for the run on small-caliber bullets was the sudden surge in gun ownership that coincided with the 2008 stock market crash and the ensuing "Great Recession." People were trying to prepare for disorder, and that meant an increase in demand for small firearms and, therefore, many more buyers of bullets.

Nominally priced at 5 cents a round, the cost of .22-caliber bullets tripled, so thousands of gun owners turned to recycling shells and learning how to make their own ammo. If things go south again, expect the cost of bullets to zoom much higher, and, potentially, for bullets to become a form of currency.

Likewise, larger-caliber bullets for shooting bigger animals will also be in demand.

Medical Supplies: A basic first-aid kit is always useful, but stockpiling burn cream, bandages, splints, medical tape, and pain relievers such as ibuprofen and acetaminophen can also put you in a good bartering position. Hospitals and medical centers might be only partially operational, and drugstores, if open, could be cleaned out.

If you can store medical supplies in bulk, consider buying some of the things that will run out quickly in an emergency, such as sterile gloves, wound dressing, antiseptic wipes, self-sticking bandages, and antibiotic creams.

Avoid drugs that have a relatively short shelf life or that need special cooled storage. Over-the-counter pain relievers, properly kept, will be in demand for years to come, as will basic stomach medications, antifungal ointments, insect repellents, and sunscreens.

Similarly, if you have access to quality prescription medications that you can stockpile, do so. Even if they expire, painkillers of a certain caliber will work better than over-the-counter meds and will therefore be in high demand.

Cigarettes and Mini Booze Bottles: Anyone who has ever watched a prison-based TV show knows that cigarettes are the currency of choice for inmates worldwide. Since prisons forbade money, cigarettes became the cash equivalent.

Like the barter currency we just described, prisoners use cigarettes to buy and sell everything they need. In an America trying to function after cash disappears, cigarettes will be just as valuable a currency outside the high walls and barbed wire as they are inside.

While it might seem improbable to use cigarettes as a currency, they do fit three out of Aristotle's four characteristics of a currency. Cigarettes are portable, easily divisible, and have intrinsic value.

However, they don't maintain their value over time. You need to spend cigarettes quickly. It takes only a couple of weeks for a cigarette to go stale once the pack is open. Try hard not to open a pack if it's not necessary. A sealed pack of cigarettes can last two to three months. You can stretch the shelf life out to a year if you keep the sealed pack of cigarettes in a freezer.

If you want an alternative that can hold value over a longer term, look for mini booze bottles, aka shooters.

Some liquor gets better as it ages, so shooters possess all four of Aristotle's qualities of a good currency.

We all know some liquor is better than others. Ensure you have the booze people actually want to drink. A shooter of Grey Goose vodka will be worth more than the generic stuff.

According to the social app BARTENDr, whiskey is the preferred liquor in 42 states. Jack Daniel's and Fireball are the most popular brands.

So if you want an alternative currency with the highest value, stick to the standards... no peach schnapps.

Wood Fuel: Gasoline is hard to keep, and the natural gas supply might be disrupted. Electricity could be spotty, too, and sooner than you think. A good long-term plan is to own remote land with trees on it. Hardwoods such as elm, hickory, oak, maple, and birch have the highest energy content in terms of Btus. Soft woods such as cedar, spruce, fir, and pine are among the lowest, but they grow faster.

If you own a forest or a large stand of trees, it's important to leave three or four mature trees standing per acre, along with a similar number of dead, fallen trees to encourage wildlife to nest and remain in the area. The ecosystem needs all of its members to allow new trees to grow and prosper, creating future forests to be cut and harvested for fuel.

"Clear-cutting" a forest might bring a higher immediate return, but it will take a very long time for the forest to recover and regrow. It equates to killing the goose for its golden eggs.

It's best to cut and split wood early in the season. Let it dry fully before burning. Wood must be split and dried over a full summer to be in the best shape for the following winter. The problem is that natural moisture in the wood makes it burn smoky and results in less efficient heat and coals that do not last.

Longtime wood collectors not only split their wood early, they also store it in the open in cords between standing trees. A properly stacked cord will protect the bulk of the wood from the elements. Consider buying a manual log splitter, axes, and sharpening tools. Splitting the logs of others could also be a useful bartering tool.

Solar Power: If you can build or cheaply purchase a small solar power station, having enough juice to recharge electronic devices could be a lifesaver. Something as simple as a solar-powered or hand-powered multiband emergency radio could matter a lot in certain situations. Indeed, running a small solar grid on your property could result in you becoming the sole supplier of power in your neighborhood.

Barter Systems: Although barter systems are often derided as impractical and inefficient, the world operated for centuries on a sophisticated system of bartering for labor, goods, and services. A rollicking "open-outcry" market of barter as a medium of exchange has sprung up in the troubled economy of modern Greece, for instance.

Today, people in Greece simply meet in town squares and advertise their skills while asking directly for what they need. Home repairs in exchange for child care, for example. Some towns have begun to operate repositories of time earned, allowing Greeks to build up a form of rudimentary credit.

Performing a task or providing a simple good earns you hours redeemable against someone else's skill or goods in the near future. It's not money, but it gets the job done. Most importantly, it's beyond government reach and tax-free.

Here are some skills that will be valuable and that you can barter for things you need:

- **Mechanic:** Repair skills will be among the most desirable talents to have in this crisis. If you are living on a tight budget, not many things will throw you off quicker than an unexpected car repair. Repairing your own car will save you hundreds of dollars, or let you barter your skills.

  Learning the basics of mechanics can be time-consuming, but once you've learned the basics, you can repair most basic faults. Vehicles all need the same kind of maintenance: oil change, air filter replacement, refrigerant for the air conditioning, etc.... Once you learn how to do these on one car, it's pretty much the same on all cars.

- **Handyman:** If you are in an urban area where cars aren't necessities, try learning some handyman skills. Knowing how to fix a leaky toilet, maintain a furnace, and repair a dishwasher motor are all valuable skills.

  Luckily, most of these are easy once you do them a couple of times. In fact, you could probably learn how a toilet works in less than five minutes and how to install a new toilet in another 10 minutes. The tricky part is actually doing it. But things get easier after a few tries.

Right now, you can learn how to fix almost anything in your home online. It only takes time and patience. You can practice these new skills in your home as things break. If online videos aren't for you, see if you can find a weekend apprenticeship with a local handyman.

- **Hunter:** In an area where hunting is a normal activity, meat will be easier to come by, as long as bullets are not in short supply. In urban areas, however, a supply of protein will be harder to replace. If the power goes down, too, there will be no way to freeze meat, so it will be important to hunt efficiently and to learn how to cure meat with salt.

For non-hunters, animal husbandry on a small scale will be a key skill. Many people are now learning how to raise chickens as a hobby.

Keeping a dozen chickens for eggs and the occasional hen for dinner could easily become a recurring form of real, tradable income. During the Great Depression, in fact, fresh eggs were used as money in some places.

If you have enough space, it can be worth considering raising rabbits and goats for their fur and meat. Pelts and skins have a long history of being forms of money in the American colonies. (That's the reason we call our dollars "bucks.")

Larger-scale farming will be harder to manage without significantly more space and access to credit, so the default form of animal-keeping is likely to involve the kinds of animals that can be kept on an acre or less of space with minimal antibiotics, veterinary care, and feed costs.

- **Butchering Skills:** One of the most distasteful aspects of our modern dietary system is the slaughterhouse. Once the economy no longer supports industrial-scale meatpacking, a very useful and appreciated skill will be the proper operation and management of an open-air abattoir.

  Farming families know all about killing poultry and hogs for food. It's a specific skill set that could translate into a significant advantage in a barter economy with fewer choices of protein supply. It isn't hard to find deer butchers in the countryside of America these days, thanks to the oversupply of deer and the growing interest in casual hunting. If you can find one, try to arrange a part-time job during hunting season in order to absorb know-how.

  It could turn out to be a tremendous boon to own the proper tools to butcher medium- to large-sized hunting kills, and to provide successful hunters with consumable cuts of their own meats. Likewise, backyard rabbit and chicken operations are not likely to want to mix the peaceful aspects of throwing feed to a few hens with the ultimate truth of having to slaughter those same hens on the same property.

- **Water Filtration:** A dollar collapse is unlikely to create significant problems in urban sanitation. However, it takes only a few boil-water orders to disrupt an entire city. Access to safe water could be at a premium in some areas. Certainly, supplies of bottled water will run out quickly. A simple water filtration kit should be stored with medical supplies and rations.

  Water from rivers and lakes is often infected with a form of micro-organism known as *Giardia lamblia*, which causes diarrhea and can lead to severe health problems. Filters can help, but boiling water is the best way to kill off waterborne organisms. It pays to understand how to build and operate a water distiller, which boils water but captures the airborne water droplets and collects them into a clean container for consumption.

Clean, drinkable water is something we tend to dismiss in the modern world, but in many countries where it is unavailable or insecure, it is literally priceless. Being able to turn questionable water into safe drinking water is a highly monetizable skill in a disrupted world.

- **Gardening:** Getting food will be the most important concern when cash and credit disappear. One way to ease this stress is to grow your own.

  Most of us don't have enough land to grow all our food, but we can definitely make a big dent in the grocery bill and maybe even have enough to barter with.

  If space is limited, find the most efficient foods to grow. People call this "intensive gardening." The typical gardener grows only one crop a year, but you can grow more. Plants have different sowing patterns and harvest times. If you plan things properly, you can get three different crops in the same space – one each in spring, summer, and fall.

  Some plants like asparagus, lettuce, and broccoli prefer cool temperatures and short days. These are perfect for the spring. Other plants like okra, squash, and tomatoes need long, hot days. Plant these in the summer. In the fall, winter squash and kale do really well. In fact, kale tastes better if it frosts briefly.

  Different climates require different plants and techniques. You can join one of 5,800 local garden clubs at www.gardenclub.org/clubs for tips from local farmers and gardeners on what to grow where and when.

- **Homegrown Spices:** Americans are fond of cooking with a variety of herbs and spices, many of which are grown and harvested in poor countries, dried, and packed into tiny glass bottles before being shipped overseas at great expense.

  In that strange system, you have an echo of a form of money that predated our modern economy and paper money – the spice trade. It was, after all, what drove Columbus to search for India by going west, leading to the discovery of America. In the chaos of an economic collapse, there is likely to be little interest in cooking or spices, but it might turn out to be worthwhile to cultivate a knowledge of basic cooking spice plants and their growing seasons on land you own.

  Oregano, for instance, is remarkably easy to grow and can survive a hard winter. Rosemary bushes grow almost nonstop. Rosemary is a very good spice for meats. Thyme is a basic spice for sauces and stews. Parsley and cilantro will grow almost anywhere and can be dried. Tarragon can be preserved in vinegar, and sage dries very well bundled. Finally, many herbs can be dried and used as teas.

  Keeping a supply of seeds on hand will be a help, too. You can buy pre-sealed packs of vegetable garden seeds that can last in storage for decades and still be ready to plant. Or you can buy smaller packets of seeds that have a shorter shelf life but are easily divisible; these can be exchanged for other goods.

- **Canning Supplies:** Canned goods could easily become a quantified medium of exchange if you store the finished goods properly and keep a supply of clear jars and materials or retrieve your jars once the food is consumed.

One way to ensure you get jars back is by incentivizing their return with credit on future canned goods, similar to the way some states collect soda bottles by allowing a few cents' credit for returning them to a store.

- **Sewing:** Being able to mend, alter, or make clothes will be a very useful – and profitable – skill.

    Often, the first thing to go on a coat is the zipper. Even if the rest of the coat is fine, it's worthless in the cold if you can't zip it up. Being able to fix that zipper saves you from having to buy a new coat. Once you get good at it, most zipper repairs can be done in under 15 minutes.

    Other mending fixes are quick and easy, too. You can sew buttons, hem pants, fix rips, and patch holes.

    In addition, making clothing can be fairly easy. It only takes a few minutes to sew two pieces of fabric together. A Sorbetto top is basically a fashionable tank top for women. You can buy the fabric for about $1. These shirts start at $7 in stores like Target and Walmart.

    Clothes aren't the only things you can make. Everyday items in every room of your house can be sewn together. Living room: curtains and couch pillows. Kitchen: oven mitts and dishrags. Bathroom: towels and washcloths. Bedroom: bed sheets and quilts.

CHAPTER 23

Financial Secrets of the Resistance

One of the most fascinating things about the many types of crisis money we've mentioned is how they come up again and again when you study the history of disaster.

In fact, one of the most valuable types of money during the Argentine crisis also saved countless lives (not to mention wealth) during the chaos of World War II.

When the Rothschild brothers escaped Nazi-occupied France for Britain, they found that the French had cut off their ability to transfer money out of the country. Fortunately, one brother was able to smuggle a few million dollars' worth of jewelry onto a cross-Channel flight. With that capital, he was able to finance his businesses and rebuild his life.

Meanwhile, the black marketeers who supplied Europe with food and clothing also used many of the items we've listed not just for barter, but also as stores of value.

In addition, they also sought out fine art, commercial and residential land (which actually outperformed farmland during the war period), and diamonds (especially useful as they were small enough to be well hidden in just about anything).

But what do you think the very best currency during that period was?

The answer may surprise you...

It was food. With food so abundant today, that may just seem impossible. But consider the case of Holland during World War II.

The Dutch were one of Europe's most important food exporters in 1939; by the mid '40s, they were starving to death.

Meanwhile, France around that time had become so rife with famine that people were getting in line to buy food as early as 3 a.m. Food became so valuable that rich French girls from good families were marrying country peasants. (It was their gardens and livestock, not their money, that the girls were after.)

Here is a list of the plants you should consider growing in your garden:

- **Black turtle or green beans**
  If you've ever eaten at a Mexican restaurant, you've likely had black turtle beans. They are highly nutritious, with one cup containing 39 grams of protein (likely more than your protein drink). Meanwhile, green beans are a great source of vitamins A, B, and K. Both are cheap and easy to grow. Green beans can be pickled.

- **Kale**
  Put aside the insufferable fad for kale today and just consider the plain facts: It has more vitamin C than an orange, contains omega-3 fatty acids, has more calcium than milk, and also contains compounds that may fight heart disease, arthritis, and cancer. Plus, it likes colder climates and can be planted in the fall.

- **Cantaloupe**
  This melon can also, surprisingly, be pickled. Not just that but it's easy to grow, easy on the stomach (for reflux sufferers and those sensitive to acidic foods), and delicious.

- **Raspberries and blackberries**
  Extremely hands-off berries to grow. You can leave 'em be for years and they won't mind. Plus, raspberries are great for arthritis and gout as they contain anti-inflammatories. They are also "chemoprotective," which means that they may reduce cancer risks.

When the ATMs Go Dark

- **Wheat or barley**
  You don't need an area the size of Kansas to plant grains. Of course, you can't plant wheat in a window planter either, but it is possible on a smaller backyard plot. Grains carry many benefits, since they're something most people don't plant. Some newer types of barley have a lower gluten content.

- **Cherry tomatoes**
  Grow them inside if you want. They are perhaps the easiest variety of tomato to grow – and one of the easiest to cook with as they require little prep. But another reason they are so beneficial is that they can be pickled for long-term conservation.

Speaking of plants, if you have the space, you might look into what some have called the "Walnut IRA."

Imagine you order a bag of $7 seeds. You drop these seeds into a spot where the earth is rich and moist, then go about your life. The years roll by, some good, some bad. Your 401(k) drops in value. Then it goes back up. Then down again. The older you get, the less predictable the world becomes.

Except for one thing: those seeds you planted.

They have now grown into dark, beautiful trees – black walnut, to be exact – and a wood so prized for its rich veneer that just one tree can be sold for as much as $20,000.

A small $10,000 investment buying a small plot of rural land, a few hundred seeds, and the necessary fertilizers, pesticides, and equipment... could turn into $140,000 by retirement.

Now, you might say that's not much better than the stock market. Of that we are not so sure. Getting the timing just right is crucial in achieving those much-lauded long-term stock gains we're always hearing about. The Dow Jones Industrial Average started with

12 stocks. Guess how many are still on there? Just one: General Electric.

Meanwhile, black walnut trees have been highly prized since at least the 1700s. Of course, nothing is risk-free. And they also require 30 years to fully grow, so the Walnut IRA is not a quick fix for a previous failure to plan for retirement. Finally, be especially wary of any "tree deals" offered by some third party who tells you to dream of big, easy profits.

But as long as you've got the time, black walnut trees are one of the most valuable things you can have. Not just that, but growing them may qualify you for tax breaks in certain states. And they are not an asset you are required to report to the government. They also make a truly special way to leave behind wealth for your kids and grandkids: a "trust" that might actually teach them a thing or two about hard work and patience.

And finally, when was the last time you saw a looter – or a government official, for that matter – carrying away a tree trunk?

CHAPTER 24

Keeping Your Money from the Government (Legally)

On a cold morning in the winter of 1998, it was hard to say who was more desperate: the terrified citizens locked in their small apartment, or the hooded men kicking their door in.

The family inside the apartment had already been cut off from their bank accounts. The money they had tied up in stock investments was as good as gone. The stock market itself had shut down after a freefall of 10% in 40 minutes.

On the other hand, the hooded officers raiding their apartment weren't much better off. Their wives, daughters, and mothers were going hungry, too, surviving on meager rations of potatoes – the only available food. Their pensions were gone. And when they weren't kicking in doors to search for "tax money" on behalf of the government, they were guarding shuttered banks in subzero weather.

Such was the state of affairs on that cold morning in the largest country in the world.

The story of how Russia came to find itself in such a crisis is longer than these pages permit. The short version is that the country got high on debt coming out of the collapse of the Soviet Union. At some point, lenders cut them off.

Governments confronted with crises of this type generally opt for the same course of action every time: confiscate and close. That is, they confiscate as much wealth as they can while simultaneously closing off escape routes out of the national money system.

In the U.S. the close phase is already happening. FATCA (Foreign

Account Tax Compliant Act) and FBAR (Foreign Bank and Financial Accounts) requirements make it so difficult to keep money in foreign bank accounts that doing so is no longer an option for most Americans. Meanwhile, banks are now required to spy on their customers and file "Suspicious Activity Reports" with the federal government.

However, there do remain a few lesser-known (yet perfectly legal) ways to get your wealth out of the federally controlled U.S. banking system. **As a reminder: You are still required to report and pay taxes on your worldwide income. And these measures do not necessarily make sense for everyone.** So please exercise caution. Talk to your financial advisors first. Consult an attorney.

With that said, let's take a look at the various ways you can move your money outside the reach of the government...

The Easiest (Even Travel-Free) Foreign Bank Accounts

The more complicated it is for the government to seize your money, the more breathing room you have in case of an emergency. Thus, even if you have to report it to the U.S. government, keeping a foreign account may come with benefits.

To that end, you could certainly just open a foreign bank account... if you can find a trustworthy bank... and if that bank allows U.S. citizens to open an account. (For example, Swiss banks no longer allow U.S. citizens. Same with Singapore.)

Here's a list of countries to consider:

- **Canada**

  <u>Benefit</u>: Very easy and the money is close at hand. Accounts are insured by the Canadian government.

  <u>Drawback</u>: If the U.S. goes down, Canada probably isn't far behind.

- **Belize**

  <u>Benefit</u>: A 9 a.m. flight from Houston arrives by noon. Or just open an account by mail.

  <u>Drawback</u>: You must do the legwork to find a trustworthy bank.

- **Andorra**

  <u>Benefit</u>: As a longtime banking haven for Europeans, Andorra comes with a sterling reputation.

  <u>Drawback</u>: Don't open an account expecting to be able to move your money around at a moment's notice. Also, it's expensive.

- **St. Vincent and the Grenadines**

  <u>Benefit</u>: Short, easy flight. Now you have a reason to visit the Caribbean.

  <u>Drawback</u>: Again, do the legwork to find a place you trust.

However, if you don't even want the government to know where your money is, you need to consider foreign safety deposit boxes and private vaults.

Hiding Your Gold

Based on the reporting requirements for FATCA and FBAR (you should check to make sure other reporting requirements don't apply to your particular situation), you can take any amount of gold, leave it in a private vault in the U.S. or abroad, and you will never need to say a word about it to the IRS or the Department of the Treasury. To be clear, we *are not* talking about a *bank* vault. Banks are required to report you.

For safety deposit boxes, there are a few requirements that must be met if you want to keep your gold hidden:

1. This only works for physical gold, not gold certificates.

2. If the safety deposit box can be accessed by a financial institution (e.g., the bank can open it and move your money around) then you may have to report it.

3. If the institution insures or offers other services for the contents of the box, you may have to report it.

4. Go to IRS.gov and find the "Comparison of Form 8938 and FBAR Requirements" page for more info.

That said, you can store gold in any foreign or domestic safety deposit box so long as the amount of gold kept in there is less than US$10,000. So imagine you want to keep a US$9,000 rainy day fund in a Canadian safety deposit box right across the border. You can absolutely do that and never say a thing about it. Just make sure you look at the bank's safety deposit agreement to ensure *they* don't forbid gold or cash being stored there.

If you want to find out more about this subject, we recommend two groups within our network: *International Living* and Banyan Hill. Tell them we sent you.

Storing Cash

Cash in a foreign currency (say Swiss francs or Canadian dollars) works the same way physical gold does (and comes with the same restrictions).

Here are a few foreign currencies you might consider:

- **Swiss franc**
  A currency that has survived two world wars in calm, stable Switzerland. On the other hand, even Switzerland has not been immune to some of the more perverse economic absurdities of late (e.g., negative interest rates).

- **Polish zloty**
  MarketWatch once called this currency "the safest major currency in Europe... and arguably in the world." We might not go that far. Eastern Europe has not historically been the most stable region in the world. Yet, with a strong economy behind it, the Polish currency is a strong contender.

- **Israeli shekel**
  If being surrounded by hostile nations in various stages of crisis hasn't been enough to ruin the Israeli shekel, we wonder what possibly could.

- **Singapore dollar**
  Think Swiss franc but without the potential liability that is being surrounded by a declining group of socialist countries.

But what about U.S. cash dollars? Opt for a private (nonbank) vault or storage unit you trust. These have no reporting requirements either way. You could store all the cash you want in one of those... if you find one you trust. Needless to say, this method would not be FDIC insured.

However, before you go flying off to the Bahamas to find a storage unit, be aware that travelling with large sums of cash sometimes requires a declaration, and even proof that you acquired it legally. Otherwise, your cash could be confiscated.

Finally, always be aware that it IS A CRIME to structure bank deposits to avoid reporting requirements. Don't give them any excuses to come for your money.

CHAPTER 25

Your Secret, Legal, and Safe Overseas Wealth Store (and How It Can Also Make You Rich)

This might just be the best way to get vast sums of money outside of the government's clutches... and keep them completely in the dark about it.

And the best part is that this asset is:

1. Indestructible,

2. Almost impossible to steal,

3. Rare (there's only a finite amount, and you can't just make more of it),

4. And has made more men billionaires than Hollywood, oil, or even Silicon Valley.

I'm talking about land. Today, you can hop across the border, store some money in a small plot of land, and never tell the U.S. government a thing.

There's a reason rich families have used land acquisition to protect themselves for generations.

There's a reason that people living in communist China plow their hard-earned cash into real estate. They don't want to wait around to see what the government does to their money.

Of course, we wouldn't recommend you buy land just anywhere. In the Third World, regime changes have been known to result in the confiscation of private property. Moreover, some countries do not allow foreigners to own property in the first place.

However, when done carefully, buying foreign land can not only be a way to store wealth outside U.S. borders, but also a way to make serious profits.

For example, from 2003 to 2015, land prices in the United Kingdom went up 300%, never mind the global financial crisis that sent housing prices crashing.

Or consider our own experience in Nicaragua. When our group of friends flew into Nicaragua around 20 years ago, we were struck by the untouched virgin beaches... the quiet, welcoming countryside... and the friendly, festive locals. Not to mention our kids discovered what is now considered one of the best surf breaks in the world.

Lots by the ocean went for less than $20,000. Today, one just listed at $450,000. That's a 2,150% return.

For comparison, since 1999, the stock market (S&P 500) has returned roughly 50%... Microsoft has returned roughly 60%... and even gold has only returned roughly 351%.

There's one more benefit to foreign land ownership: your secret foreign land holding can also act as a "Swiss bank vault" for other forms of wealth.

Remember that storing gold or cash in foreign safety deposit boxes or banks comes with some limitations. None of those apply to your own overseas land. You could bury $50,000 in cold, hard cash, gold, diamonds, fine art, whatever you want... and never have to tell a soul.

And while such a simple way of storing wealth might sound fanciful in today's world, in times of crisis, it has proved one of the best moves you can make.

As reported by Barton Biggs in his book *Wealth, War and Wisdom*:

> Swiss private bankers say that in 1939 most family fortunes
> were 20% or so in gold bars that were either in Switzerland or
> were buried in the chateau's backyard.... in the chaos of the
> last years of the war, gold buried in the backyard was a less
> dangerous, less expensive sale than any of the other alternatives
> like property or a business.

Anonymous Dollar Accounts
(Available at Your Local Pharmacy
or Grocery Store)

So you don't want to go abroad. You don't want to do anything
complex.

Here's what you can do: Get an anonymous, nearly untraceable
dollar account. After land, it is the second type of "new Swiss bank
vault" you will hear about in this book.

Now, of course, these are not bank accounts in the traditional sense.
Nor are they insured by the FDIC. You won't be able to stroll down
to your local branch and chat up the teller.

However, you will be able to place money in these accounts without
a single person knowing. Done correctly, there will be no way to
track or identify you.

Today, you are required to give your Social Security number to
get a regular bank or credit card. That same requirement goes for
reloadable cards that you might buy at a 7-Eleven or CVS.

However, at those same 7-Elevens or CVSs, or even at your local
grocery store, they also sell non-reloadable VISA, MasterCard, and
American Express "gift" cards.

You can buy these anonymously. You can get instant, easy access
to your cash and spend it nearly anywhere. One privacy-minded

software engineer, profiled by the magazine *Motherboard*, relied on $50,000 worth of these cards over 12 years.

While some cards require an address before you can use them, there is actually no requirement that the address be real. You can plug in any old name and address you please and then use the card to buy almost anything – even online.

Of course, these cards are not issued by banks. You can't go into overdraft on them. And if you lose your card, you lose your money. But in terms of accessibility and anonymity, these cards are unmatched. You can use them at the grocery store, the gas station, and even online.

Beware Your Bank: A Quick Guide to the Five Scariest Things in Your Bank Contract

No, we are not recommending you close down your bank account. We all use them. But that doesn't mean you shouldn't be mindful of what, exactly, you are agreeing to when you open an account.

Here are some common yet rather alarming provisions you might see in yours...

1. The Right for Bank Agents to Come to Your Home or Job

In 2014, the *Los Angeles Times* discovered that Capital One was including language in its contracts that allowed its agents to come find you at your home or place of business. The contracts also allowed Capital One the right to disguise its calls under any name, tricking your caller ID.

2. The Power to Freeze You Out

We all know that banks are now required to monitor their customers on behalf of the federal government. What is less commonly known is that your banks can freeze your account on their own. To do so, they must see "irregular" activity on your account. Note: That's not "illegal" activity, just "irregular," which could mean just about anything. In fact, one woman had her account frozen after inheriting $50,000.

3. Limits on Accessing Your Savings Account

The truth about savings accounts is that they are far less safe than most banks would have you believe. Reserve requirements (only 10% for most banks anyway) do not apply to savings accounts. Under federal law, you cannot take money out of a savings account more than six times in one month (unless you show up in person and demand cash). If exceeded, the bank has permission to freeze your account.

4. "Abandoned" Accounts Turned Over to the Government

You might think you can just set money in a bank and forget it. That's not always the case. If the bank deems your funds abandoned, a clause in your bank contract likely allows them to turn it over to the government. How long does it take before your funds are legally "abandoned"? Be sure to ask your bank, as that period of time will vary by state.

5. A Little-Known Clause About a Government Agency You've Never Heard Of

In your banking contract, there's likely a clause that your bank will comply and enforce all orders from an agency called OFAC. Never heard of it? OFAC has been called "the most powerful yet unknown agency in the U.S. government." Think of it like the ultimate gatekeeper to the U.S. economic system. To quote *The Wall Street Journal*, "OFAC has formidable powers: it can freeze assets [and] bar firms and individuals from the U.S. financial system." Not an agency you want to run afoul of...

CHAPTER 26

How a Gold Bug Almost
Learned to Love Cryptocurrencies...
And Why Bitcoin Is Important Now

As we continue searching for ways to move our money outside the reach of the government, we now look, reluctantly and with a good deal of squinting, at money you can't see.

We're sizing up currencies you can't feel and weighing the value of coins that have no weight at all. "Cryptocurrencies," they are called. They are the third type of "new Swiss bank vault" you will see in this book because, to some extent, they can be used and held anonymously.

Of course, the easiest (and safest) way to hold cryptocurrencies is still by using an exchange where you show your ID, just as you would in a bank.

Here's a guide from our analyst Jeff Brown to help you get started...

Cryptocurrencies 101
By Jeff Brown

Today, anytime you're stopped by the police, a TSA agent, or some other government official, they're likely – thanks to civil asset forfeiture laws – to confiscate any "suspiciously" large sums of gold or cash. What's worse, in most states, the burden of proof is on you to establish your innocence. And even if you do, what you end up with is significantly less than what was taken due to all of the costs incurred to recover your own property.

In the case of a cryptocurrency, like Bitcoin, that problem does not exist.

The "wallet" that carries your cryptocurrency exists only in cyberspace. No one can physically take it from you. You can cross borders and anonymously transfer funds to yourself or anyone else. Your money is yours to do with it as you like.

But what exactly is a cryptocurrency?

Here's Investopedia with a solid explanation:

> A digital or virtual currency that uses cryptography for security.... A defining feature of a cryptocurrency... is that... it is not issued by any central authority, rendering it theoretically immune to government interference or manipulation.

And where do they come from?

While the detailed description is far more complex than is necessary for this discussion, what is important to know is that cryptocurrencies must be "mined" into existence, just like gold. To create a unit of a cryptocurrency, a "miner" solves enough cryptographic equations to "confirm" and complete a block in the blockchain. Once a block is complete, a reward of 25 Bitcoins is issued to the miner. The reward, over time, decreases as the number of Bitcoins that have been mined nears the maximum of 21 million.

Significant capital expenditures are required in the form of expensive servers and computing systems, and large amounts of energy are needed to run these mining platforms.

As of this year, it is quite difficult to be profitable as a small-scale miner. Even the large-scale miners are typically seeing profit margins only in the single digits. The actual margins vary as the more people that mine, the harder it is to mine the coins. The system self-regulates to avoid manipulation.

Furthermore, at least in the case of Bitcoin, there is a limit to how many coins can be produced. Today, 14.3 million of the 21 million possible Bitcoins have been created. That means every additional Bitcoin is harder to mine – again, not unlike mining for gold.

In short, cryptocurrencies are not produced by a keystroke in the way that dollars are produced by the Federal Reserve; they require real-world inputs to be created.

That gives cryptocurrencies a value, flexibility, and security that even gold cannot match. And it makes them an important part of the current and future monetary discussion.

The 800-Pound Gorilla of Cryptocurrencies

In the world of cryptocurrencies, Bitcoin stands far above all others. Below, you'll see a chart of the top 10 cryptocurrencies ranked by market cap.

#	Name	Symbol	Market Cap	Price	Available Supply

#	Name	Symbol	Market Cap	Price	Available Supply
1	Bitcoin	BTC	12,831,091,720	$796.97	16,099,762
2	Ethereum	ETH	853,096,066	$9.71	87,859,193
3	Ripple	XRP	237,397,130	$0.006456	36,771,322,652
4	Litecoin	LTC	190,006,824	$3.85	49,314,379
5	Monero	XMR	152,764,048	$11.12	13,743,088
6	Ethereum Classic	ETC	103,408,999	$1.18	87,817,077
7	Dash	DASH	86,247,521	$12.28	7,024,443
8	Augur	REP	44,812,350	$4.07	11,000,000
9	MaidSafeCoin	MAID	39,389,302	$0.087038	452,552,412
10	NEM	XEM	31,940,130	$0.003549	8,999,999,999

Top 10 Cryptocurrencies as of January 13, 2017

As you can see, Bitcoin dwarfs all others. It is 15 times larger in market capitalization than No.2, Ethereum, and its next closest rival, Ripple, isn't really a competitor at all. Ripple is primarily an internet protocol that enables a currency exchange platform – essentially, a network that enables payments and transfers to be made outside of the traditional financial system.

While Ripple does have a cryptocurrency of its own, the technology is mainly used for transfers and payments that do not involve the Ripple cryptocurrency. It is a very enterprise-focused company.

Litecoin, the third-largest cryptocurrency in the world, is barely 1/67th the size of Bitcoin. After that, it is a steep slope of much smaller cryptocurrencies.

That's why Bitcoin-related companies are attracting such a tremendous amount of venture capital investment. (See the following chart.) In fact, the number of dollars flowing into this area has exceeded the amount of early-stage venture capital investing that flooded into internet technology during the key years of 1995 and 1996.

Bitcoin vs. Early Internet VC Investment

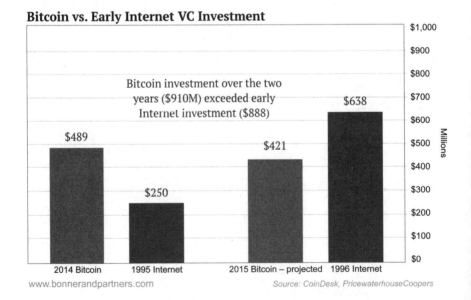

www.bonnerandpartners.com

Source: CoinDesk, PricewaterhouseCoopers

When the ATMs Go Dark

We can see clearly that in nominal terms, investment in Bitcoin-related ventures during 2014 and 2015 totaled $910 million, which was $22 million greater than the comparable investment in internet technology during 1994 and 1995.

Those numbers speak to a dramatic difference in the two technologies. That difference is even more noteworthy when you consider that it was significantly harder and more expensive to develop and produce technology during the internet's early days. The cost of starting a company and prototyping, producing, and launching a product has dropped dramatically since the mid-'90s. Today, investment dollars are dramatically more productive than they used to be, so we get significantly more leverage from invested dollars than we used to.

This is important because widespread adoption of a new form of currency requires the creation of a worldwide payment system. We'll need companies that manage, store, and secure Bitcoin wallets; companies that provide payment processing for merchants who accept Bitcoin; companies that mine Bitcoin and keep the network running; Bitcoin-based financial services companies; Bitcoin exchanges; and other infrastructure companies.

Final Thought

Investing in global currencies has long been a fairly standard approach for both investment diversification and capital appreciation. However, in an era of increasingly volatile currency swings, this practice has become more risky than it once was.

Bitcoin provides an important solution, as it is not affected by inflation, deflation, devaluation, or capital controls.

A Step-by-Step Guide to Buying Bitcoin

[**Editor's Note:** Steps will vary depending on where you're located and which bank you use.]

Step 1

Go to www.coinbase.com and enter your details – first name, last name, email, password – in the Sign Up box.

Click the blue "Sign Up" button.

Tip: I recommend a password with at least 10 characters composed of both lowercase and uppercase characters, numbers, and at least one symbol such as: # $ % & ( ) =.

You will see the word "excellent" in green if your password is considered "strong" enough, i.e., a good combination of characters that should not be easy for hackers to guess. If you don't see this, consider entering a different password.

Step 2

You will see the screen below indicating that a confirmation email will be sent to you at the email address you provided in the Sign Up box.

Go to your email account and locate the email. It should look something like the email to the right.

Click on the "Verify My Email Address" blue box. This will send an email back to Coinbase confirming your email address.

Tip: I recommend opening your email account in a different browser window so that you can leave the Coinbase screen open to return to after this step.

Step 3

Return to the Coinbase screen that you initially used to sign up on www.coinbase.com. You will see the home page of your new Coinbase Bitcoin account.

Click on the "Welcome <<your name>> – Let's get started" text link at the top of the page.

Step 4

Choose your country of residence from the drop-down list provided.

Then, enter your cell phone number in the next box.

Click the blue "Next" box.

Step 5

You will receive a text message to your cellphone with a seven-digit authentication code. Enter the code in the box on the screen to the right and click the blue "Verify Phone Number" box.

Step 6

Select the bank you would like to use to purchase your first Bitcoin. This must be a bank with which you already have an active account with online access.

Step 7a

Enter your account verification details – the username and password you use to access your online banking account with the bank selected in the previous step.

Click the blue "Next" box.

Note: Coinbase uses the most advanced security technology to keep its customers' bank account information safe. It uses an encrypted connection (SSL) which prevents third parties from intercepting any data shared by customers. It also stores all customer data with AES-256, the same advanced encryption technology used by the government.

The example shown below is for Citibank.

Step 7b

If you have multiple accounts in the bank you selected, select the account from which you would like to withdraw funds to purchase your first Bitcoin – simply click on the circular button to the left of the account you wish to select.

Click the blue "Next" box.

Step 8

To verify your identity, simply click the blue "Start Verification" box.

Step 9

In the "Country" box, enter the country in which your ID was issued.

Then, select the ID type you would like to use for verification. The most common selection is a driver's license.

Note: Coinbase uses the most advanced security technology to keep its customers' bank account information safe. It uses an encrypted connection (SSL) which prevents third parties from intercepting any data shared by customers. It also stores all customer data with AES-256, the same advanced encryption technology used by the government.

Step 10a

You can either scan your ID using your webcam, or upload a photo of it from the files on your computer. Simply click either the blue "Use webcam to scan document" button or the gray "Upload existing image" button.

Step 10b

If you have opted to upload an image of your ID from the files on your computer, you will see the screen in Step 10b on page 177.

If you do not yet have a photo of your driver's license, the easiest way is to take a photo of your license with your phone, email it to yourself, then save it as a file on your computer.

Then, click the gray "Choose File" button, and select the file from your computer to be uploaded to Coinbase.

After the photo has been uploaded, you will see the image on the screen. Click the gray "Continue" button.

If you are uploading your driver's license, you will also be asked to upload an image of the reverse side of it. Simply repeat the step above.

After the photo has been uploaded, you will see the image on the screen. Click the gray "Confirm" button.

Step 11

You will then see a screen that says "Your document has been uploaded."

Once your document has been uploaded, which can take up to one minute, a new screen will appear. You do not need to click anything here.

Step 12

Next, you will see a screen that indicates Coinbase is "Verifying Identity."

Again, you do not need to click anything. Just wait for this process to complete. It usually takes less than one minute.

Once your identity has been verified, you will receive a confirmation email like this to the email address you provided in Step 1:

Step 13

Congratulations! You are now ready to buy Bitcoin.

Once your identity has been verified, you will see the following screen for Step 13 on page 179 enabling you to purchase Bitcoin.

In the "Amount" field, you will see "USD" for U.S. dollars and "BTC" for Bitcoin.

Initially, when you are setting up your Coinbase account, there is a $25.00 limit on your initial purchase of Bitcoin.

Your payment method is pre-populated from the information you provided in a previous registration step.

I recommend you enter $25.00 in the amount field and then select the blue "Buy Bitcoin" button at the bottom of the page.

Note: You are offered the option to repeat this purchase on a regular basis (daily, weekly, etc.). I recommend you ignore this option for now. You can change your account settings at a later stage once you have completed the account setup. To ignore this option, simply leave the circular button to the left unchecked.

Step 14

You will see a final confirmation screen for your purchase. This screen summarizes your transaction and lets you know when your Bitcoins will arrive in your Coinbase account.

Select the blue "Confirm" button.

Step 15

The final screen indicates that your purchase has been completed.

There is an option to "Get your Bitcoin faster." This involves using a credit card for the purchase. I don't recommend doing this as you will be charged a handling fee – usually about 3% – for using a credit card. To skip this option, simply click on "Take me to my account," just below the blue button.

Note: It takes about three to five business days for the Bitcoin to arrive in your account when using funds from your bank account. The process is explained in this diagram:

Step 16

You will be taken to your account balance screen, which will look something like the screen in Step 16 on page 180.

If you would like to increase your daily limit for purchasing Bitcoin, click on "Settings" in the menu on the left-hand side.

Step 17

Enter your personal details, specifically your birthday and mailing address, in the fields shown.

Then, click the blue "Save" button at the bottom of the screen.

Congratulations! You have successfully set up your account and completed your first Bitcoin purchase!

Note: Online funds held by Coinbase are fully covered – through highly rated, third-party insurance firms – against any employee theft or hacking. Additionally, 98% of funds are stored offline, which provides added security against theft or loss.

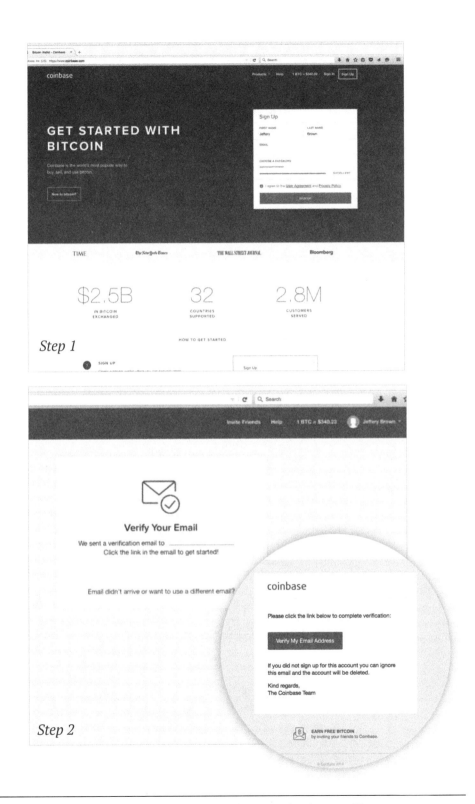

Step 1

Step 2

Step 3

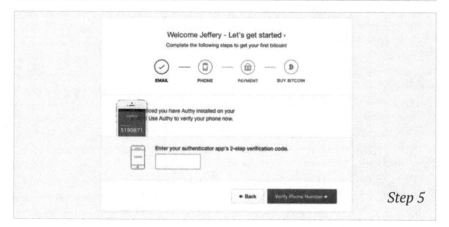

Step 4

Step 5

When the ATMs Go Dark

Step 6

Step 7a

Step 7b

Step 8

Step 9

When the ATMs Go Dark

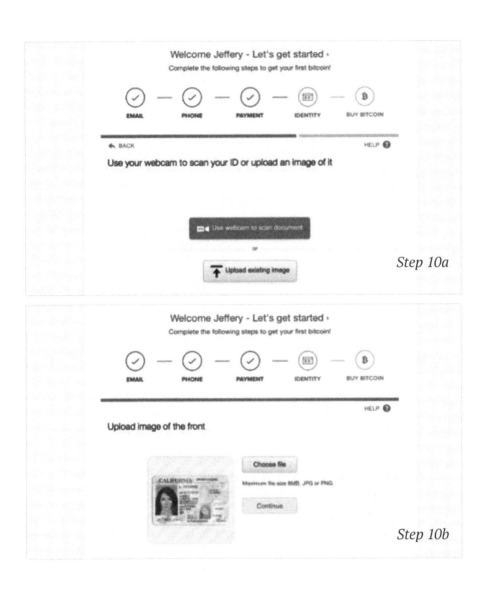

Step 10a

Step 10b

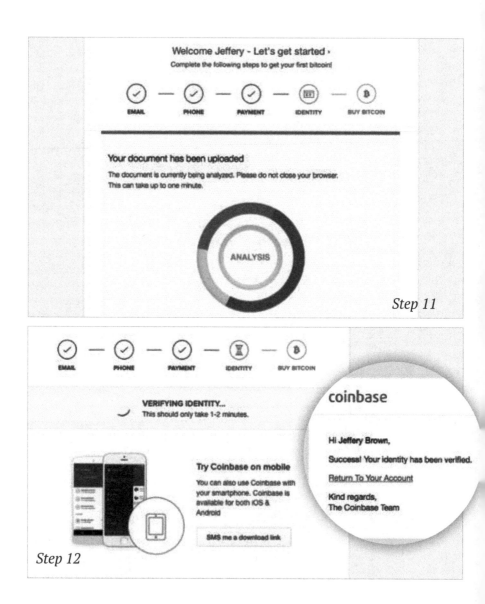

Welcome Jeffery - Let's get started ›

Complete the following steps to get your first bitcoin!

EMAIL — PHONE — PAYMENT — IDENTITY — BUY BITCOIN

Your document has been uploaded

The document is currently being analyzed. Please do not close your browser. This can take up to one minute.

ANALYSIS

Step 11

EMAIL — PHONE — PAYMENT — IDENTITY — BUY BITCOIN

VERIFYING IDENTITY...
This should only take 1-2 minutes.

Try Coinbase on mobile

You can also use Coinbase with your smartphone. Coinbase is available for both iOS & Android

SMS me a download link

coinbase

Hi Jeffery Brown,

Success! Your identity has been verified.

Return To Your Account

Kind regards,
The Coinbase Team

Step 12

EMAIL — PHONE — PAYMENT — BUY BITCOIN

Buy Bitcoin   at $336.46 per coin

Amount   MAX

USD   25.00
BTC   0.07356001

Payment method
🏦 Citi   ‡

Fee $0.25
Total $25.00

☐ Repeat this buy every   week   ‡   What's this?

Buy Bitcoin - $25.00

Step 13

EMAIL — PHONE — PAYMENT — BUY BITCOIN

Buy Confirmation

🏛 You are about to withdraw $25.00 USD from Citi

📇 0.07356001 BTC will be deposited to BTC Wallet.

📅 Your bitcoin will arrive on **Monday Nov 23, 2015.**
Learn more ›

Confirm

‹ Cancel and go back

Step 14

Complete the following steps to get your first bitcoin!

EMAIL — PHONE — PAYMENT — BUY BITCOIN

✓

Buy Completed

0.07356001 BTC will arrive in your **BTC Wallet** account on
Monday Nov 23, 2015.

Step 15

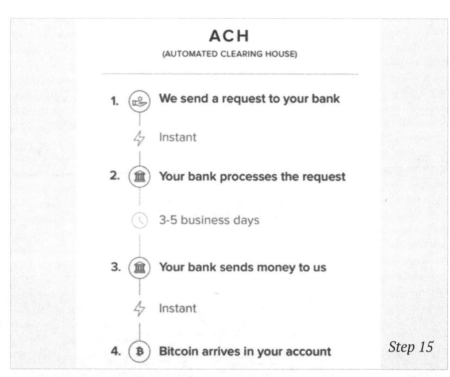

ACH

(AUTOMATED CLEARING HOUSE)

1. We send a request to your bank

Instant

2. Your bank processes the request

3-5 business days

3. Your bank sends money to us

Instant

4. Bitcoin arrives in your account

Step 15

coinbase

Invite Friends   Help   1 BTC = $336.47   Jeffery Brown

⤢ Buy/Sell Bitcoin

↗ Send/Request

🏦 Accounts

☐ BTC Wallet   0.0000 BTC
$ USD Wallet $0.00 USD
🔒 BTC Vault   0.0000 BTC

○ Settings

Free Bitcoin!   ×
Invite a friend who buys $100 of bitcoin or more, and you'll both earn $10 of free bitcoin!

Share   Tweet

Read More ›

Balance   0.0000 BTC = 0.00 USD

Wallet address

Transactions   Q Search

NOV 17   **Bought bitcoin**
0.07356001 BTC for $25.00 USD via Citi   ⓘ ARRIVES IN 5 DAYS   +0.07356001 BTC
-$25.00 USD

Step 16

Caption
Say something about yourself.

Save

Personal Details

Personal Details
Your personal information is never shown
to other users.

Legal Name

Jeffery   Brown

Date of birth

Month   ⟂   Day   ⟂   Year   ⟂

Street address 1

Street Address

Street address 2

Street Address 2

City

City

State   **Postal code**

Select state   ⟂   Postal Code

Country
United States

Save

Step 17

CHAPTER 27

Should I Be Investing?

By Bill Bonner

Great investments are not secrets that someone whispers in your ear.

Investing is a journey, not a destination. And finding good companies to buy is hard, ongoing work... the result of searching, studying, and learning.

I have been extremely fortunate. For more than 35 years, I've been paid to look. Even better, I've been able to pay others to look for me. And even with the best analysts in the world on the job, you're still never sure.

The old-timers have a saying: "You can be sure that a crackerjack analyst's luck will change the day you start following him."

There is a whole industry of analysts who try to figure out how to make above-market rates of return over a long period of time. A mountain of studies has been published. A fortune in research money has been spent.

We'll add some more to the pile.

First Principles: Think Like an Owner

In 1980, I teamed up with Mark Hulbert to launch the *Hulbert Financial Digest*, the first attempt to systematically – and more or less scientifically – track the actual results of following different investment advisers. Mark retired last year... 36 years later.

What did he discover?

"The most important lesson [of the 36 years running the newsletter] is just how difficult it is to beat the market," Hulbert said during an appearance on *MoneyLife with Chuck Jaffe*.

He was right.

Most people invest unwisely – trading in and out of faddish stocks.

Most people would be better off not trading at all and just going into an index fund, as Mark suggests, and tracking the beta return – the gain you get from just being in the market.

Can you do better than that?

After 36 years of studying the matter, Mark is not particularly optimistic. His best performer over the entire period beat the market by less than 4% per year.

Still, our research shows there are ways you can move the odds in your favor.

You can give yourself a little edge by following a few guidelines. Perhaps the most important: Think like a business owner, not an investor.

A business owner has to have his heart in it. He is concerned about the real, underlying value of his company, not necessarily current profits or the company's current stock price.

And as long as the company is headed in the right direction, he sticks with it.

In my own case, in 1984 I sold a 10% stake in my business – for just $25,000. I didn't really need the money. But I was happy to have a friend along for the ride.

One of the biggest problems you face when you start your own business are loneliness... isolation... and fear. You are marginalized. Your courage could fail... and then the business would fail with it.

My friend, now deceased, did well. Our business is still private, so I won't give numbers, but he did better than Trump... though not as well as Buffett.

Avoid Short-Termism

In the '90s, I noticed a new type of entrepreneur – especially in the tech sector. Young. Aggressive. Ambitious. His desire was to create a good business... and go to IPO as soon as possible.

Since then, I've met a few entrepreneurs who've started several successful businesses, going from one to the other like a hummingbird to honeysuckle. These serial entrepreneurs are said to have "proven" they have the knack for starting successful enterprises.

I've never believed it. My own experience is that starting one successful business is practically a miracle. More than one is probably a fraud.

The serial entrepreneur is really creating things that look like businesses... without the heart.

These businesses may be great for the entrepreneurs, promoters, venture capitalists, managers, and underwriters. But rarely for investors.

Good businesses are built by the heart, not the head... They need time, luck, perseverance, and all the other qualities that it takes to succeed in life. You can't just make them up in order to satisfy investor demand.

A real entrepreneur is one who does not identify a hot market trend; instead, it identifies him. Typically, he finds something that works for him. He puts his heart into it. Then – it turns out – it works for others, too.

Steve Jobs didn't create Apple because he thought he could make a

lot of money in the new personal computer industry. There was no
such industry. He created Apple... and that helped create the whole
industry. From the IPO in 1980 through today, the stock rose 270
times.

That's the kind of business you want to buy. And then when you are
in... stay in, unless – and until – the fundamentals change.

Our analyst Chris Mayer provides other examples of great
businesses run by real business builders:

> Howard Schultz began in 1971 in Seattle [with] a small store
> selling coffee beans, and today Starbucks is worth $76 billion in
> the stock market.
>
> Fred DeLuca's Subway began as a single sandwich shop in
> Bridgeport, Connecticut, and a $1,000 investment – and today
> generates over $9 billion in sales in over 35,000 locations.
>
> And of course, the granddaddy of the fast-food industry, Ray
> Kroc's McDonald's, which has over $5 billion in profits and is
> now the world's second-largest employer.

Here are some other examples from Chris Mayer's book
100-Baggers: Stocks That Return 100-to-1 and How to Find Them:

Company	Date Founded	Total Return	Years to 100X
Berkshire Hathaway	9/30/1965	18,261X	19.0
Kansas City Southern	12/31/1972	16,931X	18.2
Altria Group	12/31/1962	15,120X	24.2
Wal-Mart Stores	10/31/1970	12,382X	12.5
Holly Frontier	10/31/1966	12,279X	21.2
Franklin Resources	12/31/1981	11,363X	4.2
Forest Laboratories	12/31/1972	7,874X	11.5
TJX Companies	10/31/1962	6,946X	28.5
Southwest Airlines	12/31/1971	5,478X	9.5
NewMarket	12/31/1962	5,077X	22.8

I asked the question directly to Chris: How do *you* find these 100-baggers?

Here's what he said...

> The most important thing I've learned is that you have to find a really good business. McDonald's, Coca-Cola, American Express, Home Depot – these are examples of some of the greatest businesses of the 20th century.
>
> They made a high return on the capital invested in the business. And they were able to reinvest the profits back into the business and earn high returns again and again for years and years. After that, making 100x just becomes a math problem. After 25 years, a 20% annual compound return will get you 100x your money.

Of course, there's a lot more to it than a mere two paragraphs can distill. Chris also subjects stocks to a rigorous vetting system before he even considers an investment. Yet his approach has given him one of the best track records in the industry. Over the 10-year period from 2005-2015, for example, $100,000 would have turned into $480,000 – far above Hulbert's top performer.

What If the Sky Falls?

Knowing what we know about what built the modern world – phony money, runaway debt, misallocated resources, perverse and counterproductive monetary policies – we can't help but think that this is not the best time to buy U.S. equities.

But we're not foolish enough to believe we can actually foretell the future.

And for all the doom and gloom we see on the horizon, the future might not turn out so bad.

Personally, even now, I still have about one-third of my liquid wealth (not including my business and personal real estate) in stocks, heavily concentrated overseas.

I believe we are in for a rough spell, but I'm not going to take stocks completely out of my portfolio. There is almost always some room in an investment portfolio for stocks.

Maybe they'll go up. Maybe they won't. But they shouldn't be completely ignored.

When the economy is healthy and stocks are cheap... you should have 50% or more of your portfolio in them.

When the economy is fragile and stocks are expensive... you want to reduce your stock market exposure down to 30%... or even 10%, depending on your circumstances.

Generally, the more time you have (the younger you are), the more you can invest in stocks, knowing that you can recover from severe drawdowns. As you get older, or closer to the time you will need the money, the less you want to take chances. Move to gold... and cash.

Trade of the Century

Over the long term, your success depends on getting your money into the right investments – and keeping it there.

Many studies confirm that where and when you invest is much more important than the particular stocks you choose. Long-suffering readers of my newsletter, *The Bill Bonner Letter*, will recognize this as the idea that beta (allocation) beats alpha (stock selection) – first discussed in the November 2014 issue.

This is what I later tried to test and illustrate with my "Trade of the Decade" concept.

Specifically, I looked to see what was very abnormal and guessed that it would revert to the mean sometime over the following 10 years. Not especially clever. Not at all original. And certainly not an investment recommendation. Just a way to try to understand what was going on.

As some of you may recall, my first "Trade of the Decade" (buy gold; sell U.S. stocks) worked out well. I have since issued a second "Trade of the Decade" that you can read about in my newsletter. And today, I'm going to do one better... Here's my "Trade of the Century"...

The economy is barely growing, or perhaps already in recession. Prices – for assets and consumer items – are either falling... or flat. And most likely, we are headed... at least until the feds intervene in ways that are reckless and foolhardy...

So we will short credit by owning gold. But what's on the other side of the trade? What goes up? What is considered beneath contempt, neglected, and oversold?

Just as we seem to have a historic opportunity on the short side, on the long side there is one stock market that is so cheap, it alone could be worthy of the "Trade of the Century." No stock market has ever been so cheap... and survived.

Naturally, when a stock market is this cheap, it must have problems. And those problems are what you hear about. So, if you were to mention to your spouse or your financial advisor that you were investing in this stock market, they would immediately tell you that you should seek professional help... from either a certified financial planner or a psychiatrist. Maybe both.

And even I will not advise you to buy it. It's not easy to do. And it certainly is asking for trouble. Only the most intrepid and more adventuresome investors should even consider it.

Besides, who will be around in 2117 to tell me how it worked out?

Remember that the "Trade of the Century," like the "Trades of the Decade," is a learning tool... to help us understand how things work. It is not the same as serious portfolio advice.

So, with this caution, guess what stock market is so outrageously cheap... so abnormally, abysmally, absurdly cheap that it is worthy of the "Trade of the Century"...

Cyprus.

I can almost hear the gasps of disbelief.

With so many non-performing loans, Cypriot banks were in danger of going under. And since half the market stocks on the Cypriot exchange, by market capitalization, were in the financial sector, the stock market was sinking into the blue waters of the eastern Mediterranean, too.

Cyprus has the distinction of having suffered the "worst bear market in history," according to Dr. Bryan Taylor, president and chief economist of Global Financial Data.

The following chart is especially instructive. It shows what reversion to the mean looks like. And it tells us, clearly, that there's no need to worry about excess pricing in Cypriot shares today.

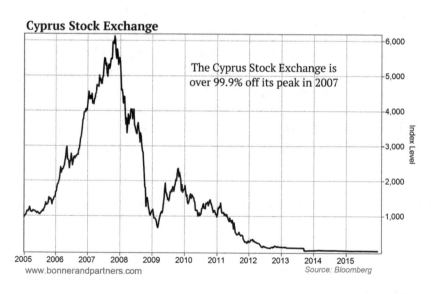

Cyprus Stock Exchange

The Cyprus Stock Exchange is over 99.9% off its peak in 2007

www.bonnerandpartners.com

Source: Bloomberg

When the ATMs Go Dar

If that were all there was to it, we wouldn't regard Cyprus as investment worthy. And perhaps it isn't. But when a stock market goes down so low, it has almost nowhere else to go but up. Cypriot stocks rose on one improbable set of circumstances and fell on another. An inflow of speculative money from Russia seems to have driven the market up to implausible heights. Then, the worldwide financial meltdown of 2008-2009 came, and the Russians ran into other problems.

The government saved the banks; it simply took depositors' money and gave it to the banks. Approximately half of all accounts over €100,000 were confiscated. I had a business account in Cyprus at the time. But it was at Barclays Bank, not a Cypriot bank. Fortunately, foreign banks were spared. But just as things go down, so, too, do they go up. And "things are looking like they might turn around for Cyprus," reports researcher Nick Rokke:

> First off, the average Cypriot was not harmed by the bail-in. It was mostly foreigners who had money invested in the banks that had the bail-ins. Locals are still spending.

> The trouble seems to be mostly contained to the financial sector. But that may be coming to an end. Right now, Cyprus is split into two countries. Southern Cyprus is controlled by those who classify themselves as Greeks. Northern Cyprus has been controlled by Turkish people since Turkey invaded in 1975.

> Turkey is still the only country that recognizes Northern Cyprus. And it has 35,000 troops stationed there. But talks of reunification are going well. If this happens, the economy is predicted to strengthen, and banks believe they can offload their non-performing loans for more than expected.

> Reunification could also expedite drilling operations in a large oil and natural gas field recently discovered off the coast. This could be a huge boon to the economy, especially if the prices of these commodities rise. While Cyprus does have a big financial

sector, its main industry is tourism – which accounts for 80% of the total economy. And tourism rose in 2015. More passengers than ever came through the airport to visit the country. But there are few ways to invest in tourism through the Cyprus stock market.

While Cyprus has been decimated by the eurozone crisis, it does appear to be turning around. It's hard to say if it will ever revert to the mean. But this country does have a history of booms and busts.

The Cyprus stock market grew by almost 1,000% in 1999, and then by 600% from 2005 to 2007. With a total capitalization of just $2 billion for the entire market, it's hard to get a sizeable investment in the country. No ETF has more than just a small percentage of its funds allocated to Cypriot companies.

The harder it is to invest in something, generally, the better the odds of success.

Right now, no one is earning much money by trying to sell Cypriot stocks to foreign investors. So, if you are going to lose money in Cypriot stocks, you'll have to do it without much help.

CHAPTER 28

Living Overseas

There are many, many reasons why you might think about going overseas, whether it's living better on less money, truly being able to retire on Social Security alone, getting great health care at a deep discount, or just removing yourself from the constant buzz of bad ideas that plague this nation like locusts.

And while it may not be for everyone, we've turned to our network of colleagues at *International Living* (which Bill founded in the 1970s), Casey Research, and Banyan Hill Publishing, we should probably for some information that could help you…

Let's start with getting a second passport, courtesy of Casey Research's **International Man** Senior Editor Nick Giambruno, a dual citizen of the U.S. and Italy who used one of the very techniques below to get Italian citizenship despite not living there.

Getting a Second Passport
By Nick Giambruno

Under Title 8 of the United States Code, a U.S. citizen who takes a second citizenship won't lose his U.S. citizenship. Two Supreme Court decisions (*Afroyim v. Rusk*, 1967, and *Vance v. Terrazas*, 1980) have upheld the permissibility of dual citizenship. A second citizenship wouldn't compromise your status as a U.S. citizen, nor would it alter your U.S. obligations in any way.

Routes to a Second Passport

There are exactly three legitimate routes to obtaining a second citizenship and passport. If you hear about a fourth route, assume that you're hearing about a scam. Black and gray market passports

---

(most commonly from Bulgaria, Mexico, Paraguay, and Cambodia) are much more trouble than they're worth and should be avoided.

Some passport scams, such as the selling of alleged "diplomatic passports," are obvious. Others that involve gray market passports are less obvious but equally dangerous.

Black market passports – stolen, cloned, or counterfeit documents – are completely illegitimate and are the stuff of organized crime and spy agencies.

While it's not impossible that you will run across black market passports in your search for a legitimate second passport, it is not very likely.

Gray market passports, on the other hand, are far more common and can appear legitimate, which makes it even more important for you to be able to identify them.

A gray market passport is an officially issued document that was obtained (usually with the help of a bribed local official) by skirting the legal requirements for naturalization. If a service provider talks about a "special friend" in a foreign government who can help you get a passport faster and easier than by following the rules, things are looking gray.

No matter the country, you should be able to point to specific naturalization laws with explicitly defined requirements that spell out everything. This information is usually located on the government's website or the website of a consulate or embassy.

If you cannot independently verify the information someone gives you with the government in question, or if what you're being told doesn't match what you know about the legal requirements, consider the discrepancy a major red flag. In all likelihood, someone is attempting to sell you a bogus passport – one that is inexpensive but dangerous and perhaps worthless.

This is especially true of providers that hype little-known economic citizenship programs. There are exactly two untroubled economic citizenship programs that have stood the test of time (see below), and they're governed by laws that are public knowledge. It's the ones that don't come with clear laws outlining the program and its costs that you have to watch out for.

Unfortunately, there is no route to obtaining a genuine second passport that is fast, easy, and cheap.

Unless you have sufficient money for an economic citizenship program, have ancestry in certain countries, or are willing to make extreme lifestyle decisions (such as marriage, adoption, or military service), expect the process to take at least three to four years. Five years is common. Ten years is not rare. Generally, faster is costlier.

Treat with skepticism anyone who claims to have a "special friend" in a foreign government who can provide a shortcut to a second passport. For more information, you can read my special report, *The Easiest Second Passport*, at http://www.internationalman.com/special-reports/on-the-ground-in-the-dominican-republic/

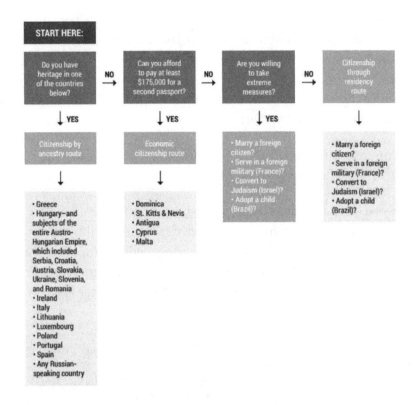

1. Citizenship by Ancestry

If you qualify, the fastest and least costly method for obtaining a second passport is through a citizenship-by-ancestry program. Within the European Union, some of the countries that offer citizenship to descendants of natives are Italy, Ireland, Poland, Greece, Lithuania, Luxembourg, Portugal, Spain, and Hungary. The latter opens the door to descendants of subjects of the entire Austro-Hungarian Empire, which included Serbia, Croatia, Austria, Slovakia, Ukraine, Slovenia, and Romania.

Russia has relaxed its requirements for obtaining citizenship for those who are fluent in Russian and live or have lived in the Soviet Union or the former Russian Empire or have parents or grandparents who lived in those areas. Get in touch with the nearest Russian embassy or consulate for details.

Each country has its own eligibility requirements and procedures. If you have an ancestor who hailed from one of those countries (usually not more remote than a great-grandparent), you should find citizenship information on the country's website, or you can visit a consulate.

If you determine that you're eligible, you will then need to give the consulate official legal and translated documents (birth, marriage, or death certificates; naturalization records; etc.) proving lineage to the relevant ancestor.

After you've submitted the complete application for citizenship, it generally will take three to six months for the consulate and government to process and approve the application. When you've become a citizen, you will then be eligible to apply for a passport.

2. Economic Citizenship Programs

Economic citizenship is the most expensive route to a second passport, but it is also the quickest. You make a substantial payment or investment, and in return the government grants you full and permanent citizenship. It all can be done in a matter of weeks, and there is no need to ever reside in the country.

The governments of Dominica and St. Kitts & Nevis (two English-speaking countries in the Caribbean) offer the only established and reliable economic citizenship programs available today. A passport from either government enables visa-free entry to most of Latin America, the Caribbean, and Europe.

The payments required under each program are detailed below. You should expect to incur additional costs, such as due diligence, background checks, processing, and other fees that all in all may exceed US$10,000 per person.

Other countries also offer economic citizenship programs. These programs, however, have not been around nearly as long as the ones from Dominica and St. Kitts & Nevis.

The lack of a reliable and stable history is an important distinction to consider between programs. Ultimately, any government has the authority to revoke the passport and/or citizenship of any of its citizens at any time for any reason, real or concocted.

An economic citizenship program must have an established record of credibility, and that comes in part from a history of domestic political acceptance. Only the St. Kitts & Nevis and Dominica programs have stood the test of time (decades) and been successfully used by thousands of people.

Dominica

The economic citizenship program of Dominica (not to be confused with the Dominican Republic) entails a nonrefundable donation to the government.

Dominica imposes an income tax on its citizens, but only if they reside in the country. Nonresident citizens are not subject to income tax.

The donation schedule is:

- US$175,000 for an individual.

- US$225,000 for a married couple.

- US$225,000 for a couple with two children under the age of 18, plus US$50,000 for each additional child.

Dominica also offers an option to invest in approved real estate projects as a path to citizenship, in addition to the donation option.

For more information, consult with the nearest consulate or embassy of Dominica.

St. Kitts & Nevis

The St. Kitts & Nevis program involves either making a donation to the government or purchasing a villa or condo from an approved developer.

If you choose the donation option, the schedule is:

- US$250,000 for a single applicant.

- US$300,000 for an applicant, spouse, and up to two children under the age of 18.

- US$350,000 for an applicant, spouse, and up to four children under the age of 18.

If you chose the real estate option, the amount you invest in approved real estate must be at least:

- US$400,000 for the applicant.

- US$25,000 for the applicant's spouse and for each dependent under the age of 18.

- US$50,000 for each dependent over the age of 18.

For dependents over 18 years of age, an additional fee of US$50,000 is payable to the government. In addition, the government requires a fee of 4%-5% of the real estate purchase price.

You must hold the property for at least five years. If you sell before that, you can lose your citizenship (and passport). Selling after five years would not compromise your status.

The real estate option entails a higher out-of-pocket cost than simply making a donation to the government. On the other hand, you would be buying something of real value (a condo on the Caribbean, for example).

St. Kitts & Nevis imposes no income tax on its citizens, i.e., there would be no tax consequences to taking up residency in the country.

Cyprus

Cyprus's economic citizenship program also gets you an EU passport, but it's a much more expensive option at a minimum of €2.5 million.

The previous minimum investment amount for obtaining Cypriot citizenship was €10 million, but following the crisis, the government cut the price and added several options. To qualify, you must have a clean criminal record and own a private residence in Cyprus worth at least €500,000.

The four paths to citizenship by investment in Cyprus are:

1. Make an investment and a donation consisting of:

    a. €2 million investment into eligible companies, and

    b. €500,000 donation to a government fund.

2. Invest €5 million in eligible companies or real estate.

3. Make a €5 million fixed-term deposit in a Cypriot bank (minimum of three years).

4. Be a person who lost €3 million from the bail-in.

3. Other Paths to Naturalization: Qualifying Circumstances

Another path to naturalization is to obtain and then maintain permanent resident status for an extended period (with or without actual presence in the jurisdiction). The required term may be as brief as three years (Paraguay) or as long as 20 years (Andorra). Most countries will grant citizenship after five years or so of permanent residency.

One qualifying circumstance is marriage, which in most cases requires you to be married for at least two years. France grants citizenship upon completion of military service. A Jewish person is eligible for Israeli citizenship, though in most cases military service will be required of any applicant over the age of 18.

The requirements for obtaining citizenship through residency vary from country to country. Some factors you should weigh in when considering a country's program are:

- Required length of residency.

- Minimum time required in-country during the residency period.

- Costs and/or mandatory investments.

- Requirement to demonstrate language proficiency.

- Permissibility of dual citizenship.

Below are details on some of the more appealing countries to consider for resident status and eventual citizenship. As a resident of a foreign country, you will likely be inducted into its tax system. Though the list is not comprehensive and the requirements are constantly changing, the material should give you a good idea of what to expect.

Countries to Consider
for Naturalization by Residency

Argentina

The Argentine constitution says that after only two years of uninterrupted permanent residency, you can become an Argentine national.

The process to apply for residency involves showing that you have enough resources to maintain yourself, or that you have been offered a job in Argentina. There are other ways as well. It can take up to two years to get permanent resident status, and then two years after that you can be eligible for Argentine citizenship.

Ecuador

Ecuador offers one of the shortest routes to naturalization. After just three years of resident status, you're eligible to be naturalized.

In total, it will take around four years when you consider the time to process the residency and naturalization requests.

You must apply for resident status while in the country and remain there for four to six weeks while your request is processed.

The easiest way to obtain resident status is to purchase a US$25,000 CD from a local bank or make a minimum US$25,000 investment in real estate. Both options require that you maintain your investment in order to keep your resident status.

During the first year of residency, you cannot be out of the country for more than 90 days. After completing the first-year residency requirement, you cannot be out of the country for more than 18 months in years two and three. After completing the three years of residency and approximately another year of processing, you become eligible for an Ecuadorian passport.

With passport in hand, you can liquidate the original US$25,000 investment and leave the country as you please.

Ecuador generally recognizes dual citizenship; you shouldn't need to give up your native passport.

Brazil

The first step toward Brazilian citizenship is to obtain resident status.

Perhaps the easiest way to obtain resident status is through the economic residency program that requires a minimum investment of 150,000 Brazilian reais in a business.

Once permanent resident status is established, the time to citizenship is four years, or less if one of the special factors below applies. Full-time residence in the country during the four years is not required. Entering the country at least once every two years is generally sufficient to maintain resident status and stay on the path to citizenship. Naturalization requires demonstrating proficiency in Portuguese.

Factors that can shorten the time to citizenship to as little as one year are:

- Marriage to a Brazilian citizen.

- Financial responsibility for a Brazilian child (most likely because you are the parent of a child born in Brazil).

- Citizenship in another country where Portuguese is an official language.

Brazil allows dual citizenship, so there is no need to give up your native passport. A Brazilian passport gives visa-free travel to many countries, which soon will include the U.S. The Brazilian government will not extradite a citizen to a foreign country for any reason.

Panama

A relatively new law (Executive Decree 343) makes obtaining permanent residency in Panama relatively easy for citizens of 47 specific countries that "maintain friendly, professional, economic, and investment relationships with the Republic of Panama." This program is often referred to as the "Specific Countries" or "Friendly Countries" program.

It requires one simple application and a deposit of at least US$5,000 in a local bank account, plus an additional sum of US$2,000 for each dependent. Applicants will also have to show proof of some meaningful economic activity in Panama, such as ownership of a Panamanian corporation or real estate, or an employment contract from a business in Panama.

Once you've obtained permanent residence, you become eligible to eventually obtain full citizenship after five years.

Eligible countries include Andorra, Argentina, Australia, Austria, Belgium, Brazil, Canada, Chile, Croatia, Cyprus, the Czech Republic, Denmark, Estonia, Finland, France, Germany, Greece, Hong Kong, Hungary, Ireland, Israel, Japan, Latvia, Liechtenstein, Lithuania, Luxembourg, Malta, Monaco, San Marino, Montenegro, the Netherlands, New Zealand, Norway, Poland, Portugal, Serbia, Singapore, Slovakia, Spain, South Africa, South Korea, Sweden, Switzerland, Taiwan, the U.S., Uruguay, and the U.K.

Although Panama does not officially recognize dual citizenship, you don't have to give up your previous passport/citizenship when you become naturalized.

Paraguay

Paraguay offers one of the easiest and cheapest ways to obtain permanent resident status and a relatively short path to naturalization.

The process for obtaining residence includes presenting a birth certificate, police record, and other documents translated into Spanish and certified to a Paraguayan consulate or embassy. After submitting the documents, the application for residency must be submitted in person in Paraguay. The applicant must also open a local bank account with at least US$5,500.

Once resident status is granted, which can take up to six months, you must be in the country to pick up your national ID card (*cédula*). The issuance of a *cédula* can take an additional two to three months.

You can apply for citizenship three years after the *cédula* has been granted. Although there's no strict requirement to live in Paraguay, it's advisable to spend some time there to demonstrate a tie to the country.

Though Paraguay prohibits dual citizenship for naturalized persons, enforcement is not consistent.

Uruguay

Obtaining resident status takes longer in Uruguay than in other Latin American countries, typically 10-12 months, and you must apply from within the country.

Presence in the country while you wait for your resident status is not required, but spending at least six months within the country is recommended.

Once you receive resident status, you can apply for naturalization after three years if you're married or five years if single. You must spend at least half of each of those years in Uruguay.

Uruguay permits dual citizenship.

***

Next up, Jessica Ramesch of *International Living* lets us in on how you can retire and run your own business in the welcoming low-tax haven of Panama.

Panama: Set Up an Overseas Business With Tax Benefits

By Jessica Ramesch

A dozen years ago, Panama was relatively unknown as a retirement destination. Few realized that the country was firmly committed to political stability and economic growth. Today, however, increasing numbers of North Americans, Europeans, and others are moving here. Some come to take advantage of the unparalleled pensioner program, which offers legal residence and a host of cost-of-living discounts to retiree residents. But many are lured by Panama's reputation as a business destination.

Panama's geographical location and newly expanded canal have helped cement the country's reputation as a leader in trade, commercial flights, and more. Organizations like Moody's have recently commended Panama for a diversified economy in which no one sector represents more than 20% of GDP. In the World Bank's 2016 *Doing Business* report, Panama ranked particularly high in the "ease of starting a business" and "trading across borders" categories.

Since 2004, Panama has had one of the world's fastest-growing economies, expanding an average of 8.4% until 2013. Despite the current global weakening, Panama will lead the region once again with growth of approximately 6% this year.

Your Income Tax Bill: Zero

In Panama, you're liable for income tax only on locally derived earnings. Your pension and any income streams from back home are 100% tax-free... and many residential properties come with tax exemptions of five to 20 years. Opening a corporation can take a matter of days, and the costs are surprisingly low. Corporations pay a capital tax (at minimum approximately US$60 on the usual capital of US$10,000), and annual registration taxes are just US$300.

Eager to attract foreign investors, Panama's government has greenlighted a number of incentives and specialized business zones.

The Colón Free Trade Zone is one of the largest duty-free zones in the world, facilitating import-export operations on every scale. The City of Knowledge – a government-sponsored cluster of companies and organizations – offers a long list of exemptions, especially for innovation, technology, and education projects.

The Epitome of Modern Urban Design

One of the world's largest and greenest mixed-development projects, Panama Pacifico is the country's newest special economic area (SEA). Located just outside the nation's capital, the vast community boasts several schools and universities as well as a growing number of retail shops, restaurants, and even medical services. Current residential offerings include everything from low-rise condo buildings to single-family homes. Live in the Town Center across from the PowerCLUB gym and Olympic-sized pool, or choose park-filled neighborhoods like Woodlands or River Valley.

Well-heeled locals and expats are already taking advantage of all this master-planned "green city" has to offer. Set up shop here and you could pay zero tax on the transfer of goods and services to ships, passengers, or ports. Though Panama Pacifico has lured plenty of big business – from giants like 3M to the Dell computer company – all are welcome. With many niches to fill, it's an optimal location for a small dry-cleaning operation, a car repair shop, or a hip little bar, barbershop, or beauty salon.

How to Pay ZERO Tax

One of the best parts about living abroad is the tax benefit.

Now, you may or may not have heard that the federal government taxes income worldwide. But there is also something known as the "Foreign Earned Income Exclusion," which allows you to exclude up to around US$100,000 (it varies with inflation) of the income you earned while your tax home was in a foreign country (i.e., for tax purposes, you were not a U.S. resident). For a helpful questionnaire to determine whether you can claim the foreign earned income exclusion, visit the IRS website.

The basic idea here is that if you live in a place like Panama – if you really reside there in a legal sense – then you can exclude up to a certain amount of the income you make in Panama. So if you make under that amount, you may owe ZERO taxes to the U.S. federal government.

A foreign-earned income tax exclusion does not affect the calculation of any self-employment tax. So you still have to pay into Medicare and Social Security if you are self-employed. However, the amount you pay will be drastically lower than any income tax you would also be forced to pay.

Of course, Panama itself may impose some taxation, which is why you might want to look into a country where there is no income tax at all... Which brings us to our next article by Ted Bauman of Banyan Hill.

***

Finally, asset protection specialist Ted Bauman of Banyan Hill Publishing reveals one of the world's best-kept secrets: the last rich, safe country where freedom still truly matters.

But first, since we are on the subject of taxes, here's a quick tip on how to virtually eliminate paying taxes altogether...

***

A Beacon of Financial Freedom in Uruguay

By Ted Bauman

I had heard the stories about a country where U.S. citizens could secure easy residence and a second passport and open a safe bank account without even acquiring residence.

Well, the stories are true. Based on my travels across the world and my visits to Uruguay, I place this country near the top of my list of most livable countries. That is mostly because of its friendly people, but also because it accords everyone the freedom to live in peace as they wish. In addition to having no restrictions on foreigners' individual ownership of land, it's one of the only countries on the planet whose constitution *guarantees* foreigners the right to live there and become citizens.

Obtaining residence and then citizenship is quick and easy. As long as you have a monthly income of at least US$1,500, all you have to do is fly to Uruguay, find a place to live, and apply for a permanent resident permit. You can stay in Uruguay while the authorities process your application, which takes from six to 12 months. You can freely leave and re-enter Uruguay, but you should spend at least six months there during this processing time.

Once you are a permanent resident, you can apply for citizenship and a Uruguayan passport in three years if you are a married couple, or in five years if you're single. What's more, that time starts to count from the day you arrive in Uruguay, regardless of when your permanent resident permit was actually granted. You don't have to give up your U.S. passport or citizenship, either.

If you want a Uruguayan passport even faster (though without citizenship), you can apply under Law 16.340. This entitles you to a passport if you invest at least US$100,000 in Uruguayan real estate or government securities. To apply for this, you must also have retirement income of at least US$1,500 a month and have Uruguayan residence.

Uruguay's benefits don't stop there. Taxes are low and apply only to income from a Uruguayan source. The law states that foreigners who relocate to Uruguay as residents do not face any extra taxes.

Uruguay remains an open economy, with no exchange controls or foreign currency limitations. In fact, 80% of bank deposits in Uruguay are held in U.S. dollars or in euros.

Political stability has been outstanding in recent decades, and Uruguay's position at the center of the Mercosur regional trade bloc (which also includes Argentina, Brazil, Paraguay, and Venezuela) has stimulated economic growth.

Uruguay's banks are among the strongest in Latin America. You don't have to live there to open an account, and there are zero capital controls or limits on how much money you can bring in or take out. Dollars and euros can be used freely and local accounts can be denominated in them. And privacy still counts... Banks in Uruguay will release information only with a court order.

Banks in Uruguay, as in many other countries, are obliged to verify both an account holder's identity and the source of the funds being placed in the account. Because of this, most banks will ask for proof of address (for example, a utility bill less than a month old), passport, a second proof of identity, reference letters from your current bank confirming that you are a reliable customer, and proof of income (such as a tax receipt or Social Security document) to open an account. You do have to visit the bank in person to open your account.

U.S. citizens looking to bank in Uruguay are best off using the state bank, Banco República, which is safe and highly reputable.

Why has Uruguay thrived where its neighbors have not? And why does it pursue such liberty, investment, and immigrant-friendly policies?

Here are three critical elements that contribute to Uruguay's stability today:

- Uruguay has been egalitarian for a long time and has a deep democratic culture. There is no large landowning class and no landless rural population.

- The population is homogenous; there are very few people who are not of European descent. This has helped Uruguay avoid the politics of racial division.

- The Uruguayan economy has evolved in such a way that the majority of the population benefits from economic freedom and export orientation. When the economy does well, everyone benefits.

Uruguay is unusual in the Latin American context. It's strongly middle class. The wealth gap is narrow, so there's no social unrest or crime fueled by angry have-nots. People work hard and there's no *mañana* attitude.

Democracy and the rule of law are well entrenched. Government is stable and transparent.

If you wish to learn more about living abroad, collecting income abroad, or obtaining a second passport, please contact our network colleagues at:

Banyan Hill Publishing – http://banyanhill.com/

Casey Research – http://www.caseyresearch.com/

International Living – https://internationalliving.com/

Tell them we sent you.

Of course, you can always follow up with our research department at Bonner & Partners for more helpful reports and contacts.

PART 5

Endgame

CHAPTER 29

The Final Act

The final act in a chess match is called the endgame.

Imagine one player has a solitary king remaining, uncaptured, on the board. According to the rules of chess, every time that king is threatened – or put in "check" – it must be moved.

When the king is threatened but cannot move anywhere else, the game is lost. This is called "checkmate."

Now, theoretically, the soon-to-be loser might move his king around forever and never get captured.

But a worthy opponent can maneuver that king into a space from which he has no hope of escape. He will put the king in check, forcing him to move... then again... then again... until the king is backed into a corner and checkmated.

This is the situation in which we find ourselves today. This is our endgame.

And we are up against the worthiest of opponents: the natural laws of money and wealth.

Of course, the play-by-play of what happens next no one can know. We can guess using years of experience in these matters, but the future remains ultimately unknowable.

Thus, this book – exhaustive as it could be – is not the end of the story. It is only the beginning of a long, strange journey on which the

American people have been unwittingly conscripted.

In the meantime, we leave you with two thoughts...

First, we live in a time when the prevailing notion in politics is that more and more comforts and luxuries should be classified as positive rights – that they should be provided and paid for by the state (i.e., by other citizens).

At the founding of the United States, only three rights were recognized at all. First iterated by John Locke, they were the right to life, the right to liberty, and the right to one's own property.

Today we add cell phones to that list. The Federal Communications Commission has classified cell phones with unlimited talk and text as a positive right. Getting one is as easy as going to freegovernmentcellphones.org.

Fast food is a positive right under the Supplemental Nutrition Assistance Program. KFC and Taco Bell both accept food stamps.

And the list goes on to include $5-a-month high-speed internet, health care, school lunches, four years of beer and fornication at a state college, low-income housing in luxury buildings with doormen, cheap energy, unions, factory jobs, high-speed rail, and of course, money itself.

In the future, we expect that the trend of expanding positive rights will see a sharp reversal.

This book is an insurance policy for just such an event.

Think of it like flood insurance. You wouldn't move to a hut in the Rocky Mountains simply because you expected a flood. But you might get some sandbags and know your evacuation routes just to be on the safe side. You would also do those things before the flood, not after it has happened and everyone is running around in a blind panic. Nothing beats careful thought and prudent behavior.

But remember, in the beginning of this book we suggested that the smart person always hedges against what he doesn't know. Remember that. In a way, this book is about hedging against society's ignorance of just how precarious our current economic situation is. But you must also take your own ignorance into account. And ours, too.

Our final parting thought is to be mindful of others. You might welcome a shutdown of our credit system, but we encourage you to remember that real people have real livelihoods, real savings, and real families at stake in this.

CHAPTER 30

How to Keep Up with the Latest in Bill's Investigation

In 1979, Bill Bonner joined two others – an Oxford scholar and the former head of the UK's BBC – to found an organization dedicated to uncovering and publishing the most radical ideas from the greatest thinkers in the country. That network now has offices on six continents and counts nearly 3 million subscribers in over 140 countries. In 1999, Bill began writing his highly respected daily column.

Recently, for the first time in his 40-year career, Bill agreed to share deeper insights with readers in a whole new way. *The Bill Bonner Letter* quickly became one of the fastest-growing newsletters in America, with readers from all walks of life, from doctors and bankers to retirees and college students.

Bill's letter isn't like a traditional investing newsletter. It's a highly unique investigation of economics, politics, world affairs, and much more... straight from the head of an organization that has predicted – with uncanny accuracy – most of the world-changing events of the past 30 years.

Bill attributes his success to employing smart, curious men and women who are not afraid to challenge accepted ideas. But, actually, many of these famous predictions have come from Bill himself...

...including his work on the Japanese crash in 1989...

...the rise of gold over 500% in the 2000s...

...the exact day of the dot-com bust...

...and the 2008 financial crisis, which he warned about no less than three times – in 2000, 2003, and 2005.

Reader James M. wrote in to say: "I am 68 and have been reading Bill for more than 20 years. He provides good common-sense perspective in a crazy world..."

Reader Ron G., who sadly lost it all in 2008, said: "I want you to know that despite being wiped out, I feel confident I will fight my way back. And you are one of the primary reasons."

"Insightful and truly outstanding," wrote James P., Esq.

"Aside from the easy-to-read, honest style, you offer very good advice and rock-solid, forthright truth. I've been a small-business owner for over 40 years or so... I know the truth when I see it," said subscriber Eric C.

To hear more from Bill, simply go to http://bonnerandpartners.com/.

We're glad you made it this far, and we look forward to hearing from you.

1 800 - 681 - 1765

45146 -

Turned to mush and muck